VERMONT HIKING

FOGHORN OUTDOORS®

VERMONT HIKING

First Edition

Michael Lanza

**AVALON
TRAVEL**

FOGHORN OUTDOORS VERMONT HIKING

First Edition

Michael Lanza

Printing History
1st edition—April 2005
5 4 3 2 1

Avalon Travel Publishing
An Imprint of
Avalon Publishing Group, Inc.

AVALON
publishing group incorporated

ISBN: 1-56691-937-1
ISSN: 1553-6092

Editor and Series Manager: Ellie Behrstock
Acquisitions Editor: Rebecca Browning
Copy Editors: Donna Leverenz
Graphics Coordinator: Deborah Dutcher
Production Coordinator: Darren Alessi
Cover and Interior Designer: Darren Alessi
Map Editors: Olivia Solís, Naomi Adler Dancis, Kat Smith, Kevin Anglin
Cartographers: Kat Kalamaras, Mike Morgenfeld

Front cover photo: Moss Glen Falls, Green Mountains, © Laurence Parent

Printed in the USA by Malloy, Inc.

About the Author

An avid four-season hiker, backpacker, climber, skier, and road and mountain biker, Michael Lanza first fell in love with hiking and the outdoors in New Hampshire's White Mountains 20 years ago. For years, he spent weekend after weekend hiking in the Whites, then branched out all over New England. During the year that he researched and wrote the first edition of *Foghorn Outdoors New England Hiking,* he figures he hiked 1,200 miles, covering all six New England states. He's now hiked and climbed extensively in the West and Northeast and as far afield as Nepal, but still returns regularly to New England to hike.

Michael is the Northwest Editor of *Backpacker* magazine and writes a monthly column and other articles for *AMC Outdoors* magazine. His work has also appeared in *National Geographic Adventure, Outside,* and other publications. He is also the author of *Foghorn Outdoors New England Hiking, Foghorn Outdoors Maine Hiking, Foghorn Outdoors Massachusetts Hiking,* and *Foghorn Outdoors New Hampshire Hiking.*

During the mid-1990s Michael syndicated a weekly column about outdoor activities in about 20 daily newspapers throughout New England and co-hosted a call-in show about the outdoors on New Hampshire Public Radio. A native of Leominster, Massachusetts, Michael has a B.S. in photojournalism from Syracuse University and spent 10 years as a reporter and editor at various Massachusetts and New Hampshire newspapers. When he's not hiking the trails of New England, he can be found in Boise, Idaho, with his wife, Penny Beach, and their son, Nate, and daughter, Alex.

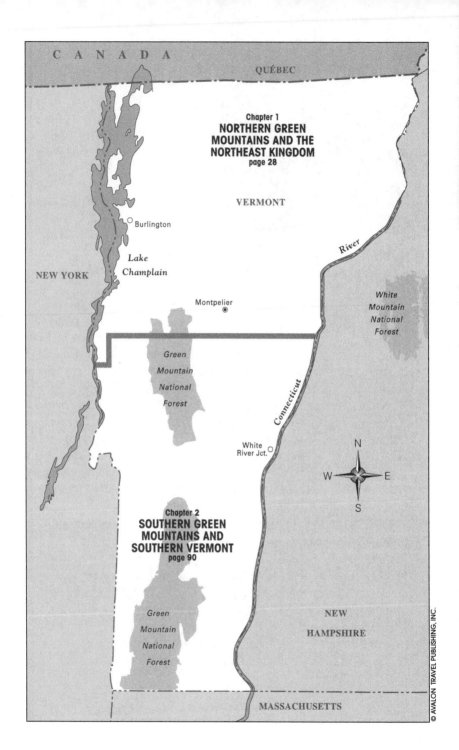

© MICHAEL LANZA

Contents

Chapter 1—Northern Green Mountains and the Northeast Kingdom

Including:
• Button Bay State Park
• Camel's Hump State Park
• Groton State Forest
• Kingsland Bay State Park
• Mount Mansfield State Forest
• Mount Philo State Park
• Putnam State Forest
• Smuggler's Notch State Park
• Underhill State Park
• Willoughby State Forest

Chapter 2—Southern Green Mountains and Southern Vermont

Including:
• Ascutney State Park
• Branbury State Park
• Coolidge State Forest
• Green Mountain National Forest
• Peru Peak Wilderness
• Quechee Gorge State Park

Resources

Index

Our Commitment

We are committed to making *Foghorn Outdoors Vermont Hiking* the most accurate and enjoyable hiking guide to the state. With this first edition you can rest assured that every hiking trail in this book has been carefully reviewed and is accompanied by the most up-to-date information. Be aware that with the passing of time some of the fees listed herein may have changed, and trails may have closed unexpectedly. If you have a specific need or concern, it's best to call the location ahead of time.

If you would like to comment on the book, whether it's to suggest a trail we overlooked, or to let us know about any noteworthy experience—good or bad—that occurred while using *Foghorn Outdoors Vermont Hiking* as your guide, we would appreciate hearing from you. Please address correspondence to:

Foghorn Outdoors Vermont Hiking, first edition
Avalon Travel Publishing
1400 65th Street, Suite 250
Emeryville, CA 94608

email: atpfeedback@avalonpub.com
If you send us an email, please put "Vermont Hiking" in the subject line.

How to Use This Book

Foghorn Outdoors Vermont Hiking is divided into two chapters, based on major regions of the state. Regional maps show the location of all the hikes in that chapter.

For Northern Green Mountains and the Northeast Kingdom trails: see pages 25–86

For Southern Green Mountains and Southern Vermont trails: see pages 87–182

There are two ways to search for the perfect hike:
1. If you know the name of the specific trail you want to hike, or the name of the surrounding geographical area or nearby feature (town, national or state park, or forest, mountain, lake, river, etc.), look it up in the index and turn to the corresponding page.
2. If you want to find out about hiking possibilities in a particular part of the state, turn to the map at the beginning of that chapter. You can then determine the area where you would like to hike and identify which hikes are available; then turn to the corresponding numbers for those hikes in the chapter.

Trail Names, Distances, and Times
Each trail in this book has a number, name, mileage information, and estimated completion time. The trail's number allows you to find it easily on the corresponding chapter map. The name is either the actual trail name (as listed on signposts and maps) or a name I've given to a series of trails or a loop trail. In the latter cases, the name is taken from the major destination or focal point of the hike.

Most mileage listings are precise, though a few are very good estimates. All mileages and approximate times refer to round-trip travel unless specifically noted as one-way. In the case of one-way hikes, a car or bike shuttle is advised.

The estimated time is based on how long I feel an average adult in moderate physical condition would take to complete the hike. Actual times can vary widely, especially on longer hikes.

What the Ratings Mean

Every hike in this book has been rated on a scale of 1 to 10 for its overall quality and on a scale of 1 to 10 for difficulty.

The quality rating is based largely on scenic qualities, although it also takes into account how crowded a trail is and whether or not you see or hear civilization.

The difficulty rating is calculated based on the following scale:

10 —The hike entails all of the following qualities: climbs 3,000+ feet in elevation, covers at least seven miles, and has rugged and steep terrain with some exposure.

9 —The hike entails at least two of the following qualities: climbs 2,500+ feet in elevation, covers at least seven miles, and/or has rugged and steep terrain with some exposure.

8 —The hike entails one or more of the following qualities: climbs 2,000+ feet in elevation, covers at least seven miles, or has rugged and steep terrain with possible exposure.

7 —The hike entails at least two of the following qualities: climbs 1,500+ feet in elevation, covers at least five miles, and/or has steep and rugged sections.

6 —The hike entails one of the following qualities: climbs 1,500+ feet in elevation, covers at least five miles, or has steep and rugged sections.

5 —The hike covers at least four miles and either climbs 1,000+ feet in elevation or has steep, rugged sections.

4 —The hike entails one of the following qualities: climbs 1,000+ feet in elevation, covers at least four miles, or has steep, rugged sections.

3 —The hike has some hills—though not more than 1,000 feet of elevation gain—and covers at least three miles.

2 —The hike either has some hills—though not more than 1,000 feet of elevation gain—or covers at least three miles.

1 —The trail is relatively flat and less than three miles.

Hike Descriptions

The description for each listing is intended to give you some idea of what kind of terrain to expect, what you might see, and how to follow the hike from beginning to end. I've sometimes added a special note about the hike or a suggestion on how to combine it with a nearby hike or expand upon your outing in some other way.

There are a couple of terms used throughout the book that reflect the land usage history in the region. Forest roads are generally dirt or gravel roads maintained by the land manager and are typically not open to motor vehicles except those of the manager. Woods roads, or "old woods roads," are abandoned thoroughfares—many were formerly public routes between colonial communities—now heavily overgrown, but recognizable as a wide path. Their condition can vary greatly.

User Groups

I have designated a list of user groups permitted on each trail, including hikers, bicyclists, dogs, horses, hunters, cross-country skiers, snowshoers, and wheelchair users.

While this book is intended primarily as a hiking guide, it includes some trails that are mediocre hikes yet excellent mountain biking or cross-country skiing routes. The snowshoe reference is intended as a guide for beginners; experienced snowshoers know that many of Vermont's bigger mountains can be climbed on snowshoes in winter, but this book indicates when snowshoeing a trail may require advanced winter hiking skills. As always, the individual must make the final judgment regarding safety issues in winter.

Wheelchair accessibility is indicated when stated by the land or facility manager, but concerned persons should call to find out if their specific needs will be met.

The hunting reference is included to remind hikers to be aware of the hunting season when hiking, and that they may be sharing a trail with hunters, in which case they should take the necessary precautions (wearing a bright color, preferably fluorescent orange) to avoid an accident in the woods. Hunting is a popular sport in Vermont and throughout New England. The hunting season generally extends from fall into early winter. The state department of fish and game and state parks and forests offices can provide you with actual dates (see Resources in the back of the book for contact information).

Access and Fees
This section provides information on trail access, entrance fees, parking, and hours of operation.

Maps
Information on how to obtain maps for a trail and environs is provided for each hike listing. When several maps are mentioned, you might want to ask the seller about a map's detail, weather-proofness, range, and scale when deciding which one to obtain. Consider also which maps will cover other hikes that interest you. Prices are usually indicative of quality and detail. I've also listed the appropriate United States Geologic Survey (USGS) map or maps covering that area. Be advised that many USGS maps do not show trails or forest roads, and that trail locations may not be accurate if the map has not been updated recently. Vermont is covered by the standard 7.5-minute series maps (scale 1:24,000). An index map also covers New Hampshire/Vermont, showing the 7.5-minute and 15-minute maps.

See Resources in the back of the book for map sources. To order individual USGS maps or the New England index maps, write to USGS Map Sales, Federal Center, Box 25286, Denver, CO 80225.

Directions
This section provides mile-by-mile driving directions to the trail-head from the nearest major town.

Contact
Most of the hikes in this book list at least one contact agency, trail club, or organization for additional information. Many hikes will give you a sample of something bigger—a long-distance trail or public land. Use the contact information to explore beyond what is found in these pages. And remember to support the organizations listed here that maintain the trails you hike.

Introduction

COURTESY VERMONT DEPARTMENT OF TOURISM & MARKETING/DENNIS CURRAN

Author's Note

Dear fellow hiker,

I have a single black-and-white photograph from what was probably my first hike up a mountain. It shows two friends and me—young, dressed in flannel shirts and jeans—standing on a rocky New England summit. In the distance, clouds blot out much of the sky. The wind lifts our hair and fills our shirts; it appears to be a cool day in early autumn.

I no longer recall what peak we hiked, only that the hike had been the idea of one of my friends; I was tagging along on an outing that seemed like something I might enjoy. In fact, my recollection of the entire day amounts to little more than a lingering sense of the emotions it generated for me—kind of an artifact of memory, like an arrowhead dug up somewhere.

I was perhaps 18 or 20 years old, and standing on top of that little mountain struck me as quite possibly the most intense and wonderful thing I'd ever done.

Of course, at that age most people have limited experience with things intense and wonderful. But I found that as my fascination with high places grew, so did the inspiration that began on that first summit.

I have since done much hiking all over Vermont and the rest of New England and taken my thirst for that feeling to bigger mountains out West—hiking, backpacking, and climbing in the Sierra Nevada, the Cascades and Olympics, the Tetons and Wind River Range, the Rockies from Colorado to Alberta, and Alaska. My work allows me to spend many days and nights every year in wild country.

When asked to write *Foghorn Outdoors New England Hiking,* I realized I would spend a summer hiking trails I had not yet visited but which belong in a guide this comprehensive. While I expected to sorely miss the West, where I'd been spending summers hiking and climbing, instead I found myself enjoying a reunion of sorts with my hiking roots. I finally got to many places that had been on my checklist for some time. And, to my surprise, the hikes I relished most were those I had known the least about, those scattered trails that for various reasons attract relatively few hikers.

Foghorn Outdoors Vermont Hiking is the product of many days on the trail and a reflection of many personal memories. As you use it to explore Vermont's trails, I urge you to walk lightly, to do your part to help preserve these fragile places, and to venture beyond the popular, well-beaten paths to lesser-known destinations.

I also invite you to let me know about any inaccuracies by writing to my publisher, Avalon Travel Publishing, at the following address: Foghorn Outdoors Vermont Hiking, Avalon Travel Publishing, 1400 65th Street, Suite 250, Emeryville, CA 94608.

I hope this book helps you find the same kind of experiences I have enjoyed in these mountains and forests—to discover your own arrowhead.

—*Michael Lanza*

Vermont Overview

Like no other state in New England, Vermont is defined by its mountains. Hikers travel from many parts of the country to see Vermont's famous hills, especially during the fall foliage season.

The Green Mountains run the length of the state, rolling up from round, forested hills in the south to the taller, sometimes craggy peaks in the state's midsection and on to the rambling hills and peaks of the north country. The Green Mountains are the locus of much of the state's hiking—the 350,000-acre Green Mountain National Forest has 500 miles of hiking trails.

Running for about 270 miles along the Green Mountains' spine, from the edge of Massachusetts to the Canadian border, the Long Trail (LT) is the nation's first long-distance hiking trail. Although an estimated 60–80 people through-hike the Long Trail every year, countless day hikers access parts of the trail.

Hikes in the Northern Green Mountains and Northeast Kingdom region vary in character from short, easy walks by the shore of Lake Champlain to ambitious jaunts up the state's highest peaks. Some of these hikes are very popular, others more remote and obscure or simply too rugged to attract many hikers. You can find whatever you want in this part of the state: trails and summits as challenging as anything in New England, and quiet, easy trails where you don't have to work hard for great views.

Southern Vermont's mountains and hills tend toward a gentler topography that's as scenic as it is kinder to knees and leg muscles. Being a bit closer to population centers of southern New England and New York, these southerly trails can attract crowds at times. But they're also a good training ground for hikers aspiring to greater challenges—and a great place to pass an afternoon, day, or weekend.

The Appalachian Trail

Perhaps the most famous hiking trail in the world, the Appalachian Trail (AT) runs 2,174 miles from Springer Mountain in Georgia to Mount Katahdin in Maine, along the spine of the Appalachian Mountains in 14 states.

About 150 miles of the Appalachian Trail pass through southern Vermont (more than 100 miles of it coinciding with Vermont's Long Trail). Among the highlights of the Green Mountain State's portion of the Appalachian Trail are Killington Peak, Stratton Mountain and Stratton Pond, and the view from Glastenbury Mountain's fire tower.

A few hundred people hike the entire Appalachian Trail end to end every year, but countless thousands take shorter backpacking trips and day hikes somewhere along the Appalachian Trail. Well maintained by various hiking clubs that assume responsibility for different sections, the trail is well marked with signs and white blazes on trees and rocks, or cairns above treeline. Shelters and campsites are spaced out along the Appalachian Trail so that backpackers have choices of where to spend each night, but those shelters can fill up during the busy season of summer and early fall, especially on weekends.

The prime hiking season for the Appalachian Trail in Vermont generally runs from June through October.

Hiking Tips

Climate

With Vermont's peaks arrayed north-south and varying significantly in elevation and latitude, eager hikers can often find someplace to hike virtually year-round—or a trail to snowshoe or cross-country ski. But the wildly varied character of hiking opportunities here also demands some basic knowledge of and preparation for hitting the trails.

Vermont's prime hiking season stretches for several months from spring through fall. September is often the best month for hiking, with dry, comfortable days, cool nights, and few bugs. Fall foliage colors peak anywhere from mid-September or early October. The period from mid-October into November offers cool days, cold nights, no bugs, few people, and often little snow.

Any time of year, average temperatures typically grow cooler as you gain elevation or move northward. In general, summer high temperatures range 60–90°F with lows from 50°F to around freezing at higher elevations. Days are often humid in the forests and lower elevations and windy on the mountaintops. July and August see occasional thunderstorms, but July through September are the driest months.

Black flies, or mayflies, emerge by late April or early May and pester hikers until late June or early July, while mosquitoes come out in late spring and dissipate (but do not disappear) by midsummer.

In the higher peaks of Vermont's Green Mountains, high-elevation snow disappears and alpine wildflowers bloom in late spring; by late October, wintry winds start blowing and snow starts flying (though it can snow above 4,000 feet in any month of the year). Spring trails are muddy at low elevations—some are closed to hiking during the April–May "mud season"—and buried under deep, slushy snow up high, requiring snowshoes. Winter conditions set in by mid-November and can become very severe, even life-threatening. Going above tree line in winter is considered a mountaineering experience by many (though these mountains lack glacier travel and high altitude), so be prepared for harsh cold and strong winds.

In the smaller hills and flatlands, the snow-free hiking season

Cross-Country Skiing and Snowshoeing

Many hikes in this book are great for cross-country skiing or snowshoeing in winter. But added precaution is needed. Days are short and the temperature may start to plummet by mid-afternoon, so carry the right clothing and don't overestimate how far you can travel in winter. Depending on snow conditions and your own fitness level and experience with either snowshoes or skis, a winter outing can take much longer than anticipated—and certainly much longer than a trip of similar distance on groomed trails at a cross-country ski resort. Breaking your own trail through fresh snow can also be very exhausting—take turns leading, and conserve energy by following the leader's tracks, which also serve as a good trail to return on.

The proper clothing becomes essential in winter, especially the farther you wander from roads. Wear a base layer that wicks moisture from your skin and dries quickly (synthetics or wool, not cotton), middle layers that insulate and do not retain moisture, and a windproof shell that breathes well and is waterproof or water-resistant (the latter type of garment usually breathes much better than something that's completely waterproof). Size boots to fit over a thin, synthetic liner sock and a thicker, heavyweight synthetic-blend sock. For your hands, often the most versatile system consists of gloves and/or mittens that also can be layered, with an outer layer that's water- and windproof and preferably also breathable.

Most importantly, don't overdress: Remove layers if you're sweating heavily. Avoid becoming wet with perspiration, which can lead to you cooling too much. Drink plenty of fluids and eat snacks frequently to maintain your energy level; feeling tired or cold on a winter outing may be an indication of dehydration or hunger.

As long as you're safe, cautious, and aware, winter is a great time to explore New England's trails. Have fun out there.

often begins by early spring and lasts into late autumn. Some of these trails are even occasionally free of snow during the winter, or offer opportunities for snowshoeing or cross-country skiing in woods protected from strong winds, with warmer temperatures than you'll find on the bigger peaks up north.

For more information about weather-related trail conditions, refer to the individual hike listings.

Basic Hiking Safety

Few of us would consider hiking a high-risk activity. But like any physical activity, it does pose certain risks, and it's up to us to

ⓕ First-Aid Checklist

Although you're probably at greater risk of injury while driving to the trail-head than you are on the trail, it's wise to carry a compact and lightweight first-aid kit for emergencies in the backcountry, where an ambulance and hospital are often hours, rather than minutes, away. Many are available at outdoor gear retailers. Or prepare your own first-aid kit with attention to the type of trip, the destination, and the needs of people hiking (for example, children or persons with medical conditions). Pack everything into a thick, clear plastic resealable bag. And remember, merely carrying a first-aid kit does not make you safe; knowing how to use what's in it does.

A basic first-aid kit consists of:

- ❑ 2 large cravats
- ❑ 2 large gauze pads
- ❑ 4 four-inch-square gauze pads
- ❑ 1 six-inch Ace bandage
- ❑ roll of one-inch athletic tape
- ❑ several one-inch adhesive bandages
- ❑ several alcohol wipes
- ❑ safety pins
- ❑ tube of povidone iodine ointment (for wound care)
- ❑ Moleskin or Spenco Second Skin (for blisters)
- ❑ knife or scissors
- ❑ paper and pencil
- ❑ aspirin or an anti-inflammatory medication
- ❑ SAM splint (a versatile and lightweight splinting device available at many drug stores)
- ❑ blank SOAP note form

minimize them. For starters, make sure your physical condition is adequate to your objective—the quickest route to injury is overextending either your skills or your physical abilities. You wouldn't presume that you could rock climb a 1,000-foot cliff if you've never climbed before; don't assume you're ready for one of Vermont's hardest hikes if you've never—or not very recently—done anything nearly as difficult.

Build up your fitness level by gradually increasing your workouts and the length of your hikes. Beyond strengthening muscles, you must strengthen the soft connective tissue in joints like knees and ankles that are too easily strained and take weeks or months to heal from injury. Staying active in a variety of activities—hiking, running, bicycling, Nordic skiing, etc.—helps develop good overall fitness and decreases the likelihood of an overuse injury. Most importantly, stretch muscles before and after a workout to reduce the chance of injury.

Vermont's most rugged trails—and even parts of its more moderate paths—can be rocky and steep. Uneven terrain is often a major contributor to falls resulting in serious, acute injury. Most of us have a fairly reliable self-preservation instinct—and you should trust it. If something strikes you as dangerous or beyond your abilities, don't try it, or simply wait until you think you're ready for it.

An injury far from a road also means it may be hours before the victim reaches a hospital. Basic training in wilderness first aid is beneficial to anyone who frequents the mountains, even recreational hikers. New England happens to have two highly respected sources for such training, and the basic course requires just one weekend. Contact SOLO (Conway, NH; 603/447-6711, website: www.solo schools.com) or Wilderness Medical Associates (Bryant Pond, ME; 888/945-3633, website: www.wildmed.com) for information.

Clothing and Gear

Much could be written about how to outfit oneself for hiking in Vermont, with its significant range of elevations and weather, a few alpine zones, huge seasonal temperature swings, and fairly wet climate. But in the simplest of terms, you should select your clothing and equipment based on:

- the season and the immediate weather forecast
- the amount of time you plan to be out (a couple of hours, a full day, more than one day)
- the distance you'll be wandering from major roads
- the elevation you will hike to
- the abilities of your hiking companions

At lower elevations amid the protection of trees or on a warm day, you may elect to bring no extra clothing for an hour-long outing, or no more than a light jacket for a few hours or more. But higher elevations, especially above tree line, get much colder than the valleys—

about three degrees Fahrenheit per thousand feet—and winds can grow much stronger. Many a Green Mountains hiker has departed from a valley basking in summer-like weather and reached a summit wracked by wintry winds and lying under a carpet of fresh snow, even during the summer months. Insulating layers, a jacket that protects against wind and precipitation, a warm hat, and gloves are always a good idea when climbing Vermont's highest peaks.

The most important piece of gear may be well-fitting, comfortable, supportive shoes or boots. Finding the right footwear requires trying on various models and walking around in them in the store before deciding. Everyone's feet are different, and shoes or boots that feel great on your friend won't necessarily fit you well. Deciding how heavy your footwear should be depends on variables like how often you hike, whether you easily injure feet or ankles, and how much weight you'll carry. Generally, I recommend hiking in the most lightweight footwear that you find comfortable and adequately supportive.

Above all, use good judgment and proceed with caution. When you're not sure, take the extra layer of clothing, just in case.

Foot Care

At an Appalachian Mountain Club seminar on winter backpacking that I attended years ago, one instructor told us that, besides the brain, "Your feet are the most important part of your body." Hurt any other body part and you might conceivably still make it home under your own power. Hurt your feet, and you're in trouble.

Take care of your feet. Wear clean socks that wick moisture from your skin while staying dry. If you anticipate your socks getting wet from perspiration or water, bring extra socks; on a multiday trip, have dry socks for each day, or at least change socks every other day. Make sure your shoes or boots fit properly, are laced properly, and are broken in if they require it. Wear the appropriate footwear for the type of hiking you plan to do.

Whenever I stop for a short rest on the trail—even if only for five or 10 minutes—I sit down, pull off my boots and socks, and let them and my feet dry out. When backpacking, wash your feet at the end of the day. If you feel any hot spots developing, intervene before they progress into blisters. A slightly red or tender hot spot can be protected from developing into a blister with an adhesive bandage, tape, or a square of moleskin.

If a blister has formed, clean the area around it thoroughly to avoid infection. Sterilize a needle or knife in a flame, then pop and drain the blister to promote faster healing. Put an antiseptic ointment on the blister. Cut a piece of moleskin or Second Skin (both of which have a soft side and a sticky side with a peel-off backing) large enough to overlap the blistered area. Cut a hole as large as the blister out of the center of the moleskin, then place the moleskin over the blister so that the blister is visible through the hole. If done properly, you should be able to walk without aggravating the blister.

Water and Food

Streams and brooks run everywhere in Vermont. If you're out for more than a day in the backcountry, finding water is rarely a problem (except on ridgetops and summits). But protozoans and bacteria occur in backcountry water sources, and campers do not always maintain an appropriate distance between their messes and the stream. Assume you should always treat water from backcountry sources, whether by using a filter or iodine tablets, boiling, or another proven method. Day hikers will usually find it more convenient to simply carry enough water from home for the hike.

Most of us require about two liters of water per day when we're not active. Like any physical activity, hiking increases your

 Green Mountain Club

The Green Mountain Club (GMC) maintains Vermont's Long Trail and the numerous shelters and camping areas along it. These shelters include lean-tos with one open side, similar to those found along the Appalachian Trail, and enclosed cabins, or lodges, most of which are on the trail's northern half. Where the Long Trail crosses private land, camping is prohibited except at Green Mountain Club cabins and shelters. The water sources at most shelters and camping areas are usually reliable, though this is never guaranteed in a dry season. Green Mountain Club caretakers collect an overnight fee for staying in its shelters; see individual hike listings for details.

For more information, contact the Green Mountain Club at 802/244-7037, website: www.greenmountainclub.org.

body's fluid needs by a factor of two or more. On a hot, sticky summer day, or even on a cold, dry winter day (when the air draws moisture from your body even though you may not be perspiring), you'll need even more water than you would on a cool autumn afternoon. A good rule of thumb for an all-day hike is two liters of water per person, but that could even leave you mildly dehydrated, so carry a third liter if you think you may need it. Dehydration can lead to other, more serious problems, like heat exhaustion, hypothermia, frostbite, and injury. If you're well hydrated, you will urinate frequently and your urine will be clear. The darker your urine, the greater your level of dehydration. If you feel thirsty, dehydration has already commenced. In short: Drink a lot.

Similarly, your body burns a phenomenal amount of calories walking up and down a mountain. Feed it frequently. Carbohydrates like bread, chocolate, dried fruit, fig bars, snack bars, fresh vegetables, and energy bars provide a source of quick energy. Fats contain about twice the calories per pound than carbs or protein, and provide the slow-burning fuel that keeps you going all day and warm through the night if you're sleeping outside; sate your need for fats by eating cheese, chocolate, canned meats or fish, pepperoni, sausage, or nuts.

Animals

While the mountains and forests of Vermont have a variety of wildlife, including black bears and even the occasional moose (not to mention more rare species like wildcat and bald eagle), for the most part, you don't have to worry for your safety in the backcountry. In years of hiking, I've never encountered a bear on the trail, though I've seen scat and other signs of their presence.

Still, a few sensible precautions are in order. If you're camping in the backcountry, know how to hang or store your food properly to keep it from bears and smaller animals like mice, which are more likely to be a problem. If you're fortunate enough to see a moose or bear, you certainly should never approach either. These creatures are wild and unpredictable, and a moose can weigh several hundred pounds and put the hurt on a much smaller human.

The greatest danger posed by wildlife is that of hitting an animal while driving on dark back roads at night, which can wreck vehicles and injure people. At night, drive more slowly than you would during daylight.

Low-Impact Practices

Many of Vermont's trails receive heavy use, making it imperative that we all understand how to minimize our physical impact on the land. The nonprofit organization Leave No Trace (LNT) advocates a set of principles for low-impact backcountry use that are summarized in these basic guidelines:

• Plan ahead and prepare
• Travel and camp on durable surfaces
• Dispose of waste properly
• Leave what you find
• Minimize campfire impact
• Respect wildlife
• Be considerate of other visitors

Below are more-specific recommendations that apply to many backcountry areas:

• Choose a campsite at least 200 feet from trails and water sources, unless you're using a designated site. Make sure your site bears no evidence of your stay when you leave.
• Avoid building campfires; cook with a backpacking stove.
• Carry out everything you carry in.
• Do not leave any food behind, even buried, as animals will dig it up. Learn how to hang food appropriately to keep it from bears. Black bears have spread their range over much of New England in recent years, and problems have arisen in isolated backcountry areas where human use is heavy.
• Bury human waste beneath six inches of soil at least 200 feet from any water source. Burn and bury, or carry out, used toilet paper.
• Even biodegradable soap is harmful to the environment, so simply wash your cooking gear with water away from any streams or ponds.

- Avoid trails that are very muddy in spring; that's when they
  are most susceptible to erosion.
- And last but not least, know and follow any regulations for
  the area you will be visiting.

LNT offers more in-depth guidelines for low-impact camping
and hiking on its website, www.lnt.org. You can also contact
them by mail or phone: Leave No Trace Inc., P.O. Box 997, Boulder, CO 80306; 303/442-8222 or 800/332-4100, website:
www.lnt.org.

Trail Etiquette

One of the great things about hiking—at least for as long as I've
been hiking—has always been the quality of the people you meet
on the trail. Hikers generally do not need an explanation of the
value of courtesy, and I hope that will always ring true.

Personally, I yield the trail to others whether I'm going uphill
or down. All trail users should yield to horses by stepping aside
for the safety of everyone present. Likewise, horseback riders
should, whenever possible, avoid situations where their animals
are forced to push past hikers on very narrow trails. Mountain
bikers should yield to hikers, announce their approach, and pass
non-bikers slowly. During hunting season, non-hunters should

wear blaze orange, or an equally bright, conspicuous color. Most of the hunters I meet are responsible and friendly and deserve like treatment.

Many of us enjoy the woods and mountains for the quiet, and we should keep that in mind on the trail, at summits, or backcountry campsites. Many of us share the belief that things like cell phones, radios, CD players, and hand-held personal computers do not belong in the mountains; if you must use them, use discretion.

This region has seen some conflict between hikers and mountain bikers, but it's important to remember that solutions to those issues are never reached through hostility and rudeness. Much more is accomplished when we begin from a foundation of mutual respect and courtesy. After all, we're all interested in preserving and enjoying our trails.

Large groups have a disproportionate impact on backcountry campsites and on the experience of other people. Be aware of and respect any restrictions on group size. Even where no regulation exists, keep your group size to no more than 10 people.

Dogs can create unnecessary friction in the backcountry. Dog owners should respect any regulations and not presume that strangers are eager to meet their pet. Keep your pet under physical control whenever other people are approaching.

Best Hikes in Vermont

Can't decide where to hike this weekend? Here are my picks for the best hikes in several categories:

Top Trails for Fall Foliage Viewing

Jay Peak, Northern Green Mountains and the Northeast Kingdom, page 30. Autumn colors arrive early this far north, often by late September.

Mount Hunger, Northern Green Mountains and the Northeast Kingdom, page 54. Try this trail in the fall for a dazzling display, or in winter for views of snow-capped peaks.

Camel's Hump, Northern Green Mountains and the Northeast Kingdom, page 59. Spectacular foliage is the payoff for those who tackle this difficult climb in the autumn.

Griffith Lake and Baker Peak, Southern Green Mountains and Southern Vermont, page 155. Baker Peak, though just 2,850 feet high, thrusts a rocky spine above the trees for great views of the wooded valley embracing the little town of Danby.

Stratton Mountain and Stratton Pond, Southern Green Moun-

a backpacker on the Long Trail on Camel's Hump

tains and Southern Vermont, page 172. Not for the faint of heart, the observation tower at the top of Stratton Mountain provides expansive views and a place to catch your breath.

Top Hikes to Waterfalls

Laraway Lookout, Northern Green Mountains and the Northeast Kingdom, page 32. A short distance from this hike's start, the Long Trail passes picturesque cascades.

Texas Falls Nature Trail, Southern Green Mountains and Southern Vermont, page 111. At Texas Falls, Texas Brook blasts through a narrow, spectacular gorge spanned by a wooden bridge with an excellent view of the gorge.

Falls of Lana and Rattlesnake Cliffs, Southern Green Mountains and Southern Vermont, page 113. The beautiful Falls of Lana tumble well over 100 feet through several picturesque cascades and pools.

Top Hikes to Lakes and Swimming Holes

Kingsland Bay State Park, Northern Green Mountains and the Northeast Kingdom, page 72. This one-mile loop ventures out onto a point jutting into massive Lake Champlain.

Button Bay State Park, Northern Green Mountains and the Northeast Kingdom, page 74. This flat, one-mile walk leads to Button Point, where a finger of rock thrusts into Lake Champlain: The views take in a wide sweep from Camel's Hump and the Green Mountains to the east to the Adirondacks across the lake.

Skylight Pond, Southern Green Mountains and Southern Vermont, page 105. This 4.8-mile round-trip hike is an easy day trip, but many take advantage of the nearby lodge to stretch this into an overnighter.

Big Branch Wilderness, Southern Green Mountains and Southern Vermont, page 152. Two of this hike's highlights are water: the roaring, rock-strewn bed of the Big Branch and placid Griffith Lake.

Stratton Mountain and Stratton Pond, Southern Green Mountains and Southern Vermont, page 172. Stratton Pond, the largest body of water on the Long Trail, is encircled by a 1.5-mile trail.

Top Easy Backpacking Trips

The Long Trail: U.S. 4 to Route 73, Brandon Gap, Southern Green Mountains and Southern Vermont, page 121. This 20-mile, relatively flat Long Trail section passes through dense, quiet woods.

Big Branch Wilderness, Southern Green Mountains and Southern Vermont, page 152. A 14-mile trek with good fishing opportunities en route.

Stratton Mountain and Stratton Pond, Southern Green Mountains and Southern Vermont, page 172. Overnight hikers can choose to camp at the North Shore tenting area or to stay the night at the Stratton shelter.

Glastenbury Mountain, Southern Green Mountains and Southern Vermont, page 178. A good two-day trip punctuated with an overnight stay at the roomy Goddard shelter.

The Long Trail: Massachusetts Line to Route 9, Southern Green Mountains and Southern Vermont, page 180. Although this hike is more than 14 miles in length, the flat terrain makes it a good choice for novice backpackers.

Top Difficult Backpacking Trips

The Long Trail: Route 17, Appalachian Gap, to the Winooski River, Northern Green Mountains and the Northeast Kingdom, page 76. Camel's Hump is the prize, but the rest of this hike is filled with wonderful surprises.

The Monroe Skyline, Northern Green Mountains and the Northeast Kingdom, page 82. Professor Will Monroe knew what he was doing when he was the catalyst for relocating the Long Trail onto this scenic ridge crest—now the trail's finest stretch.

The Long Trail: Lincoln-Warren Highway, Lincoln Gap, to Route 17, Appalachian Gap, Northern Green Mountains and the Northeast Kingdom, page 84. This 11.6-mile stretch traverses the high, narrow ridge of Lincoln Mountain, passing over several summits, including spectacular 4,006-foot Mount Abraham. It's also the middle portion of the fabled Monroe Skyline.

The Long Trail: Route 125, Middlebury Gap, to the Lincoln-Warren Highway, Lincoln Gap, Southern Green Mountains and Southern Vermont, page 101. This fairly rugged, 17.4-mile Long Trail stretch passes over nine named 3,000-foot peaks, with several good, long views of the Green Mountains.

The Long Trail: Route 103 to U.S. 4, Southern Green Mountains and Southern Vermont, page 137. For northbound hikers, here's where the Long Trail gets rough, culminating at the rocky crown of Killington Peak.

Top Hikes for Children

Stowe Pinnacle, Northern Green Mountains and the Northeast Kingdom, page 52. Let your kids forge the trail by spotting the blue blazes that mark this relatively easy hike.

Mount Hunger, Northern Green Mountains and the Northeast Kingdom, page 54. It's a good climb for two miles uphill for stout young legs, but this summit feels like an accomplishment and has some of the best views in Vermont.

Mount Philo, Northern Green Mountains and the Northeast Kingdom, page 57. A two-mile loop takes in the dramatic views of the Green Mountains and Adirondacks from the clifftop.

Deer Leap Mountain, Southern Green Mountains and Southern Vermont, page 124. This three-mile round-trip to open ledges feels like a mountain to young hikers.

Quechee Gorge, Southern Green Mountains and Southern Vermont, page 130. A two-mile loop with very little climbing involved explores this spectacular, 150-foot-deep gorge.

Top Summit Hikes

Jay Peak, Northern Green Mountains and the Northeast Kingdom, page 30. At 3,861 feet and very near the Canadian border, Jay Peak is one of the more remote higher mountains along

family hiking on the summit of Mount Mansfield

the Long Trail, overlooking a vast North Country of mountains, forest, and few roads.

Mount Mansfield via any trail, Northern Green Mountains and the Northeast Kingdom, page 42. Vermont's highest peak offers a long, alpine summit ridge with long views of the Green Mountains, White Mountains, Lake Champlain, and the Adirondack Mountains.

Camel's Hump via any trail, Northern Green Mountains and the Northeast Kingdom, page 59. A 4,083-foot peak with views of the Adirondacks, Lake Champlain, the Green Mountains, and the Whites, many consider this Vermont's finest summit.

Mount Abraham, Southern Green Mountains and Southern Vermont, page 93. One of only four mountains in Vermont to rise above tree line, this peak offers a stunning 360-degree view.

Killington Peak via any trail, Southern Green Mountains and Southern Vermont, page 132. Vermont's second-highest peak, 4,241-foot Killington boasts one of the finest panoramas in the state.

Top Hikes for Solitude and Remoteness

Laraway Lookout, Northern Green Mountains and the Northeast Kingdom, page 32. Along the less-visited northern tier of the Long Trail, this spot offers a long view of mountains and the Champlain Valley.

Mount Mansfield: Hell Brook and Cliff Trails, Northern Green Mountains and the Northeast Kingdom, page 45. Tackling some of the region's most rugged terrain, this hike rarely sees many people beyond Mansfield's popular summit.

Mount Hunger, Northern Green Mountains and the Northeast Kingdom, page 54. Link Mount Hunger to Stowe Pinnacle via a somewhat rugged ridge trail through lush subalpine forest along the Worcester Range.

The Long Trail: Route 17, Appalachian Gap, to the Winooski River, Northern Green Mountains and the Northeast Kingdom, page 76. While solitude is a rare find atop Camel's Hump, much of this 18.4-mile leg of the Long Trail can actually feel pleasantly lonely and remote.

Shrewsbury Peak, Southern Green Mountains and Southern Vermont, page 140. With long views of Franconia Ridge in the White

Mountains, Mount Ascutney, Mount Monadnock, and the Green Mountains, it's surprising how few hikers visit this summit.

Top Short, Scenic Walks

Prospect Rock, Northern Green Mountains and the Northeast Kingdom, page 38. A hike of less than a mile reaches this spot overlooking the Lamoille River Valley and the Sterling Range.

Smuggler's Notch, Northern Green Mountains and the Northeast Kingdom, page 40. Long a route for illegal trade, today this notch is a pleasant spot for a stroll among massive boulders and steep cliffs.

Camel's Hump View, Northern Green Mountains and the Northeast Kingdom, page 68. Stroll an easy 0.2 mile round-trip for a striking view of Camel's Hump.

Robert Frost Interpretive Trail, Southern Green Mountains and Southern Vermont, page 107. Here's a nice, flat, one-mile loop through forest, marsh, brooks, and a meadow with a view of the Green Mountains.

Quechee Gorge, Southern Green Mountains and Southern Vermont, page 130. An easy, two-mile loop explores this spectacular gorge.

Top Hikes Along Mountain Ridges

Mount Mansfield: Sunset Ridge and Laura Cowles Trails, Northern Green Mountains and the Northeast Kingdom, page 42. Ascend Vermont's tallest peak via the thrillingly exposed Sunset Ridge, but be prepared for gusty winds.

Camel's Hump: Long Trail/Bamforth Ridge, Northern Green Mountains and the Northeast Kingdom, page 62. The most arduous trail up 4,083-foot Camel's Hump, this passes numerous open ledges with the most sustained views of any route on the mountain.

The Monroe Skyline, Northern Green Mountains and the Northeast Kingdom, page 82. More than 47 miles of the Long Trail follow this scenic ridge crest, the trail's most spectacular stretch.

The Long Trail: Lincoln-Warren Highway, Lincoln Gap, to Route 17, Appalachian Gap, Northern Green Mountains and the Northeast Kingdom, page 84. For nearly 12 miles, the Long Trail traverses the high, narrow ridge of Lincoln Mountain.

Mount Wilson, Southern Green Mountains and Southern Vermont, page 97. This Long Trail stretch leads to ledges near Wilson's summit (3,745 feet) with one of the finest views on the Long Trail—the long chain of the Green Mountains stretching southward.

Top Hikes for Rugged Mountain Terrain

Mount Mansfield: Sunset Ridge and Laura Cowles Trails, Northern Green Mountains and the Northeast Kingdom, page 42. This loop features lots of hiking up steep, rocky terrain.

Mount Mansfield: Hell Brook and Cliff Trails, Northern Green Mountains and the Northeast Kingdom, page 45. Not all of New England's tough trails are found in the White Mountains—this ascent covers some of the region's most rugged terrain.

Camel's Hump: Monroe/Alpine Trails Loop, Northern Green Mountains and the Northeast Kingdom, page 65. This 6.6-mile hike loops over the mountain's rugged summit.

Mount Abraham, Southern Green Mountains and Southern Vermont, page 93. The 360-degree view from this summit is earned via steep, rugged trail.

Top Hikes to Watch the Sunrise

Prospect Rock, Northern Green Mountains and the Northeast Kingdom, page 38. Hike less than a mile to this overlook with a big view south of the Lamoille River Valley and the Sterling Range.

Skylight Pond, Southern Green Mountains and Southern Vermont, page 105. Ease into the morning here after slumbering in comfort at the Skyline Lodge.

Mount Ascutney, Southern Green Mountains and Southern Vermont, page 142. You'll have to start hiking very early, by headlamp, to catch the sunrise from Ascutney's summit, but the long views in all directions make it a worthwhile effort.

Bromley Mountain from Mad Tom Notch, Southern Green Mountains and Southern Vermont, page 163. The summit observation deck offers one of the better views on the southern portion of the Long Trail. Hiking there from the Mad Tom Notch is slightly shorter, with much less vertical gain, than from Route 11/30.

Glastenbury Mountain, Southern Green Mountains and Southern Vermont, page 178. With an overnight stay at the roomy Goddard shelter, you can make the short hike to Glastenbury's summit fire tower for a 360-degree panorama of the southern Green Mountains as the first rays of morning sun rake across them.

Top Hikes to Watch the Sunset

Mount Philo, Northern Green Mountains and the Northeast Kingdom, page 57. The westward panorama from these cliffs includes sprawling views of Lake Champlain and the Adirondacks.

Silent Cliff, Southern Green Mountains and Southern Vermont, page 109. Few sunsets will be as dramatic as one from this ledge jutting out into thin air, with its broad view of Middlebury Gap and west to the Champlain Valley and the Adirondacks.

Falls of Lana and Rattlesnake Cliffs, Southern Green Mountains and Southern Vermont, page 113. From Rattlesnake Cliffs, the view extends westward to the Adirondacks.

Deer Leap Mountain, Southern Green Mountains and Southern Vermont, page 124. The westward panorama from these cliffs includes sprawling views of Lake Champlain and the Adirondacks.

Mount Ascutney, Southern Green Mountains and Southern Vermont, page 142. Sunset is easier to catch than a sunrise from Ascutney's summit, and the views extend as far as the White Mountains and Green Mountains.

Chapter 1

© MICHAEL LANZA

Northern Green Mountains and the Northeast Kingdom

Northern Green Mountains and the Northeast Kingdom

Roughly half of the 23 hikes in this chapter are along the northern portion of the 270-mile Long Trail, which runs the length of the Green Mountains from Massachusetts to the Canadian border; the others include short, easy, and scenic walks along Lake Champlain and on lower hills with views of the Green Mountains, as well as a few hikes in the rural forests of the Northeast Kingdom. The northernmost hikes in this chapter—Jay Peak, Mounts Pisgah and Hor, Laraway Lookout, and Prospect Rock—are among the most remote and least-traveled trails in New England, and good places to escape the crowds.

Some of Vermont's highest, most rugged, and most challenging and enjoyable peaks—including Camel's Hump and Mount Mansfield—are featured in this chapter. Camel's Hump and several other summits lie along the famed Monroe Skyline, the Long Trail's most spectacular stretch.

In the Green Mountain National Forest, no-trace camping is permitted, dogs must be leashed, and hunting is allowed in season, but not near trails.

The prime hiking season begins in late spring, when higher-elevation snows have melted away and lower-elevation mud has dried up, and lasts until the leaves hit the ground, usually in early October (though all of October can provide some great cool-weather hiking with a small chance of snow). To prevent erosion, parts of the Long Trail are closed to hiking during mud season, roughly mid-April through Memorial Day. Where the Long Trail crosses private land, camping is prohibited except at the Green Mountain Club cabins and shelters. Winters are long and cold throughout Vermont—although there's great ski touring and snowshoeing to be had—and road access through the mountain passes is never assured (the Lincoln-Warren Highway through Lincoln Gap is not maintained in winter).

In Vermont's more than 50 state parks, trails are closed mid-April through mid-May (the lower-elevation state park trails dry out sooner than higher parts of the Long Trail). At all state park main entrances, a fee is collected from Memorial Day through Columbus Day ($2.50 per person age 14 and older, and $2 for children ages 4–13). A free, basic trail map is available at virtually all state parks, or from the Vermont Department of Forests, Parks, and Recreation (see Resources in the back of the book).

Hunting is allowed in virtually all state parks and forests during hunting seasons, which are in the fall. Mountain bikes are allowed only on designated trails, which are few; consult with park officials for current designated trails. Dogs are not allowed in day-use areas such as picnic areas, but are unrestricted on trails.

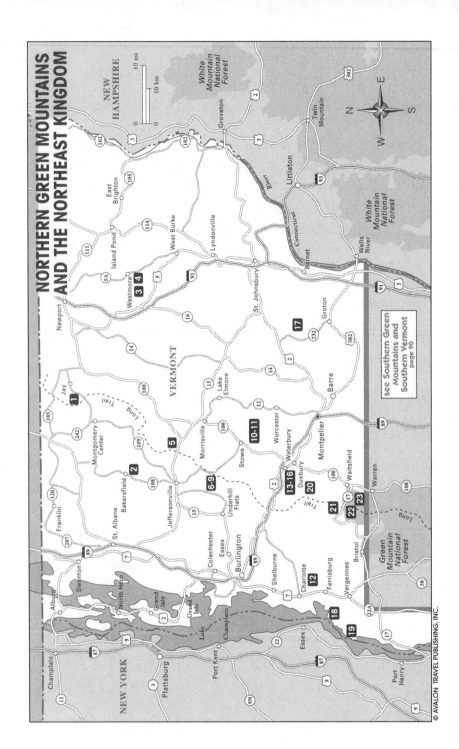

NORTHERN GREEN MOUNTAINS AND THE NORTHEAST KINGDOM

see Southern Green Mountains and Southern Vermont page 90

© AVALON TRAVEL PUBLISHING, INC.

Contents

1 JAY PEAK

between Jay and Montgomery Center

Total distance: 3.4 miles round-trip   **Hiking time:** 2.5 hours

Difficulty: 6   **Rating:** 9

At 3,861 feet in elevation and just 10 trail miles from the Canadian border, Jay Peak is one of the more remote large mountains along the entire 270-mile length of the Long Trail. The views from the summit—where there are buildings belonging to the Jay Peak Ski Area—are of a vast North Country of mountains, forest, and few roads. And just about half of what you see lies in Canada. Remember that winter arrives earlier here than on peaks farther south. My wife, her dad, and I hiked up here once in the first week of November to find lots of ice and a snow dusting the trail. This hike climbs almost 1,700 feet.

From the turnout, cross the highway and follow the white blazes of the Long Trail northbound. You immediately pass the small lean-to known as Atlas Valley shelter—not designed for overnight use. In 0.1 mile, the Jay Loop Trail, also a part of the Catamount ski trail, branches left, leading 0.2 mile to the Jay Camp cabin. Just 0.3 mile farther up the Long Trail, you pass the north end of the Jay Loop. The Long Trail ascends steadily onto the mountain's southeast ridge. Just over a mile from the road, you start getting obstructed views to the south and west through the subalpine forest. The wooded peak to the west, connected to Jay by a high ridge, is Big Jay, at 3,800 feet one of New England's 100 highest summits and a destination for hikers seeking to tick off that list. In recent years, a trail was cut to Big Jay. At 1.5 miles from the highway, the Long Trail crosses a ski resort trail and then climbs over open, rocky terrain the final 0.2 mile to the summit. Descend the way you came.

User Groups

Hikers and dogs. Dogs must be leashed. No wheelchair facilities. This trail should not be attempted in winter except by hikers prepared for severe winter weather, and is not suitable for bikes, horses, or skis. Hunting is allowed in season unless otherwise posted.

Access and Fees

Parking and access are free. This Long Trail section is on private land. Camping is prohibited except at the Green Mountain Club cabins and shelters. The Jay Camp cabin is located 0.3 mile north of Route 242 and 1.6 miles south of the Jay Peak summit, 0.2 mile off the Long Trail. The Laura Woodward shelter lies 1.5 miles north of Jay Peak, on the Long Trail. The Atlas Valley shelter is a small lean-to a few steps north of Route 242 on the Long Trail; exposed to winds, it does not provide good overnight shelter.

Maps

The waterproof *End-to-End Map of the Long Trail* is available for $8.95 from the Green Mountain Club. For a topographic area map, request Jay Peak from USGS Map Sales, Federal Center, Box 25286, Denver, CO 80225, 888/ASK-USGS (888/275-8747), website: http://mapping.usgs.gov.

Directions

Park in a large turnout where the Long Trail crosses Route 242, 6.5 miles east of the junction of Routes 242 and 118 in Montgomery Center, and 6.5 miles west of the junction of Routes 242 and101 in Jay.

Contact

Green Mountain Club Inc., 4711 Waterbury-Stowe Road, Waterbury Center, VT 05677, 802/244-7037, website: www.greenmountainclub.org.

❷ LARAWAY LOOKOUT
between Waterville and Belvidere Junction

Total distance: 3.6 miles round-trip   **Hiking time:** 2.5 hours

Difficulty: 6   **Rating:** 9

I hiked to Laraway Lookout on an early November day that felt decidedly wintry, with an inch of snow on the ground and icicles hanging from cliffs along the trail. At the lookout, clouds obscured any view for several minutes. But patience rewarded me, for the clouds eventually separated, showing me the long view to the southwest and west of mountains and the Champlain Valley. This hike climbs about 1,500 feet.

From the parking area, follow the white-blazed Long Trail northbound. The wide path crosses a brook in 0.1 mile and then follows its opposite bank for about 200 yards, turning sharply left near picturesque cascades. The Long Trail ascends gradually through woods, growing more rugged for the final 0.3 mile, passing beneath dramatically overhanging cliffs and climbing a narrow, rocky gully before reaching the open ledge at Laraway Lookout. The wooded summit of Laraway Mountain lies just 0.4 mile farther up the Long Trail, but this hike returns the way you came.

User Groups
Hikers and dogs. Dogs must be leashed. No wheelchair facilities. This trail may be difficult to snowshoe, in part because of severe winter weather, and is not suitable for bikes, horses, or skis. Hunting is allowed in season unless otherwise posted.

Access and Fees
Parking and access are free. This Long Trail section is on private land. Camping is prohibited except at the Green Mountain Club cabins and shelters. The Corliss Camp is three miles north of Laraway Lookout on the Long Trail.

Maps
The waterproof *End-to-End Map of the Long Trail* is available for $8.95 from the Green Mountain Club. For a topographic area map, request Johnson from USGS Map Sales, Federal Center,

Box 25286, Denver, CO 80225, 888/ASK-USGS (888/275-8747), website: http://mapping.usgs.gov.

Directions

From Route 109, 1.8 miles north of the Waterville Market in the town center and 8.8 miles south of the junction of Routes 109 and 118 in Belvidere Corners, turn east onto Codding Hollow Road. Drive 1.4 miles and bear left at a fork and a sign for Long Trail parking. A mile farther, the road narrows to a two-track that may not be passable in mud season. Follow that two-track for 0.2 mile to a dirt parking lot on the left.

Contact

Green Mountain Club Inc., 4711 Waterbury-Stowe Road, Waterbury Center, VT 05677, 802/244-7037, website: www.greenmountainclub.org.

3 MOUNT HOR

in Willoughby State Forest

Total distance: 2.8 miles round-trip   **Hiking time:** 1.5 hours

Difficulty: 2   **Rating:** 8

Lake Willoughby is a long finger of water embraced on both sides by the sheer cliffs of Mount Hor to the west and Mount Pisgah to the east. Tucked away in Vermont's remote Northeast Kingdom, Willoughby's topography inspires images of a Norwegian fjord more than it does the bucolic farmland and forests surrounding Willoughby State Forest. It certainly evoked that image for me one raw, rainy day I spent hiking Mounts Hor and Pisgah (see next listing). This is a great hike for viewing the fall foliage, which normally peaks by late September this far north. Although the views from 2,656-foot Mount Hor are not as nice as they are from Mount Pisgah, Hor does have beautiful views and is easier to hike than Mount Pisgah because much of the elevation is gained while driving the CCC Road to the trailhead. The actual hike climbs less than 500 feet.

From the parking area, walk 40 feet farther up the road and turn right onto the Herbert Hawkes Trail. In another 30 feet, turn right with the trail onto an old logging road. The hike is easy and nearly flat for the first 0.4 mile, passing through several wet, muddy areas. The road eventually narrows to a trail, then swings left, and ascends the mountainside. At 0.7 mile you reach a trail junction marked by signs: To the left it is 0.3 mile to the wooded, viewless summit of Mount Hor (not included in this hike's distance); for this hike, turn right and follow the fairly easy trail another half mile to the first overlook of Lake Willoughby and Mount Pisgah, and 0.1 mile beyond that to the second overlook. After you've taken in the views, hike back along the same route to the parking area.

User Groups

Hikers and snowshoers. No wheelchair facilities. This trail is not suitable for bikes, horses, or skis. Dogs are not allowed in day-use areas such as picnic areas, but are unrestricted on trails. Hunting is allowed in season.

Access and Fees

Parking and access are free. Trails are closed during the spring mud season, usually mid-April to mid-May, and are posted when closed for peregrine falcon nesting in spring.

Maps

The *Northern Vermont Hiking Trail Map,* which covers Mount Mansfield, Camel's Hump, Lake Willoughby (including Mounts Hor and Pisgah), Cotton Brook, Little River, the Worcester Range (including Stowe Pinnacle and Mount Hunger), and Mount Elmore, is available from the Green Mountain Club for $4.95. For a free, basic map of hiking trails, contact the Vermont Department of Forests, Parks, and Recreation. For topographic area maps, request Sutton and Westmore from USGS Map Sales, Federal Center, Box 25286, Denver, CO 80225, 888/ASK-USGS (888/275-8747), website: http://mapping.usgs.gov.

Directions

Take I-91 to Exit 25 for Barton. Turn right off the ramp onto Route 16 east. Drive one mile into Barton and turn right, then go 0.2 mile and turn left, staying on Route 16 east. Follow Route 16 for another 7.2 miles to the north end of Lake Willoughby and turn right onto Route 5A south. Drive 5.7 miles, beyond the foot of the lake, and turn right onto the gravel CCC Road beside a dirt parking lot. Follow that road for 1.8 miles to a parking area on the right.

Contact

Vermont Department of Forests, Parks, and Recreation, 103 South Main Street, Waterbury, VT 05671-0601, 802/241-3655, website: www.state.vt.us/anr/fpr.

4 MOUNT PISGAH

in Willoughby State Forest

Total distance: 3.8 miles round-trip   **Hiking time:** 2.5 hours

Difficulty: 6   **Rating:** 9

See the Mount Hor trail notes (previous listing) for more descriptive information about the Willoughby State Forest. This hike up Mount Pisgah climbs about 1,500 feet. From the parking area, cross the highway to the South Trail, which begins at a sign reading "Willoughby State Forest Trailhead." The trail soon crosses a swampy, flooded area on a boardwalk and then starts climbing a wide path well marked with blue blazes. After about 0.7 mile, you pass the first of three successive lookouts on the left with partly obstructed views of Lake Willoughby and Mount Hor, the third lookout being the best among them. At one mile, you reach a short side path leading left to Pulpit Rock, with an excellent view of the lake. Some hikers may choose to turn back from here, for a round-trip of two miles.

Continue up the trail, scrambling up rock slabs 0.5 mile beyond Pulpit Rock, and then watch for a side path leading to the right about 100 feet to a view southeast to New Hampshire's White Mountains. Return to the South Trail, turn right, and continue to Mount Pisgah's 2,756-foot summit, 1.9 miles from the road. Three side paths around the wooded summit lead left to ledges atop tall cliffs with sweeping views of Lake Willoughby and Mount Hor. A sign points to the last side path, the north overlook. Head back the way you came.

User Groups

Hikers and snowshoers. No wheelchair facilities. This trail is not suitable for bikes, horses, or skis. Dogs are not allowed in day-use areas such as picnic areas, but are unrestricted on trails. Hunting is allowed in season.

Access and Fees

Parking and access are free. Trails are closed during the spring mud season, usually mid-April to mid-May, and are posted when closed for peregrine falcon nesting, usually in spring.

Maps

The Northern Vermont Hiking Trail Map, which covers Mount
Mansfield, Camel's Hump, Lake Willoughby (including Mounts
Hor and Pisgah), Cotton Brook, Little River, the Worcester
Range (including Stowe Pinnacle and Mount Hunger), and
Mount Elmore, is available from the Green Mountain Club for
$4.95. For a free, basic map of hiking trails, contact the Vermont
Department of Forests, Parks, and Recreation. For topographic
area maps, request Sutton and Westmore from USGS Map
Sales, Federal Center, Box 25286, Denver, CO 80225, 888/ASK-
USGS (888/275-8747), website: http://mapping.usgs.gov.

Directions

Take I-91 to Exit 25 for Barton. Turn right off the ramp onto
Route 16 east. Drive one mile into Barton and turn right, drive
0.2 mile, and turn left, staying on Route 16 east. Follow Route
16 for another 7.2 miles to the north end of Lake Willoughby
and turn right onto Route 5A south. Drive 5.7 miles, beyond the
foot of the lake, to a dirt parking lot on the right.

Contact

Vermont Department of Forests, Parks, and Recreation, 103
South Main Street, Waterbury, VT 05671-0601, 802/241-3655,
website: www.state.vt.us/anr/fpr.

5 PROSPECT ROCK
in Johnson

Total distance: 1.6 miles round-trip   **Hiking time:** 1 hour

Difficulty: 2   **Rating:** 8

This relatively easy hike—it climbs about 500 feet over less than a mile—winds along a more remote Long Trail stretch, leading to a bucolic view of a northern Vermont farming valley and its surrounding hills. From the turnout, follow the Long Trail white blazes northbound up the dirt road for about 0.1 mile and then turn left with the trail into the woods. The Long Trail follows an old woods road and then swings right onto a footpath winding uphill and reaching Prospect Rock, 0.8 mile from the parking area. Its open cliff-top ledges overlook the Lamoille River Valley and the Sterling Range to the south. Follow the same route back.

User Groups
Hikers and dogs. Dogs must be leashed. No wheelchair facilities. This trail may be difficult to snowshoe and is not suitable for bikes, horses, or skis. Hunting is allowed in season unless otherwise posted.

Access and Fees
Parking and access are free. This Long Trail section is on private land. Camping is prohibited except at the Green Mountain Club cabins and shelters. The Roundtop shelter is located 1.8 miles north of Prospect Rock on the Long Trail.

Maps
The waterproof *End-to-End Map of the Long Trail* is available for $8.95 from the Green Mountain Club. For a topographic area map, request Johnson from USGS Map Sales, Federal Center, Box 25286, Denver, CO 80225, 888/ASK-USGS (888/275-8747), website: http://mapping.usgs.gov.

Directions
From Route 15, two miles west of the junction of Routes 15 and 100C in Johnson, and immediately east of the Lamoille River

bridge, turn north onto a secondary road at signs for the Long Trail and Waterville. Continue 0.9 mile to a turnout on the right, across the road from the Ithiel Falls Camp Meeting Ground. You see the Long Trail's white blazes on rocks at the turnout. Do not block the dirt road with your vehicle.

Contact

Green Mountain Club Inc., 4711 Waterbury-Stowe Road, Waterbury Center, VT 05677, 802/244-7037, website: www.greenmountainclub.org.

6 SMUGGLER'S NOTCH

in Smuggler's Notch State Park between Stowe
and Jeffersonville

Total distance: 0.2 miles round-trip   **Hiking time:** 0.25 hour

Difficulty: 1   **Rating:** 9

Historically, the notch served as the route for illegal trade with
Canada after President Thomas Jefferson's 1807 embargo for-
bade American trade with Great Britain and Canada, creating a
hardship for northern Vermonters. It also was used as an escape
route to Canada for fugitive slaves, and, once an improved road
was built through the notch in 1922, served as a route for smug-
gling liquor from Canada during Prohibition.

During the warm months, this hike is an easy walk around the
height of land in Smuggler's Notch, where massive boulders line
the narrow, winding roadway and lie strewn throughout the
woods. Tall cliffs flank the notch to either side, making it look
more like the White Mountains than the usually more tame
Green Mountains.

From the south end of the parking turnout, follow a short but
obvious path about 200 feet back into the jumble of garage-sized
boulders known as Smuggler's Cave, reputedly a stash for contra-
band during the War of 1812. Then wander around the notch;
you'll see the white blazes of the Long Trail enter the woods
across the road, a short distance uphill from the turnout. In winter, this hike transforms into a more involved outing, not to mention one typically accompanied by a frigid wind. With Route 108
not maintained through the notch, you have to hike or cross-
country ski up to the height of land—about a mile at an easy to
moderate grade from the Jeffersonville side, and about 2.3 miles
from the Stowe side, which is much steeper. But the notch makes
for a scenic ski tour and a fun descent.

User Groups

Hikers, skiers, and snowshoers. No wheelchair facilities. This
trail is not suitable for horses. Mountain bikes are allowed only
on designated trails, which are few; consult with park officials for
current designated trails. Dogs are not allowed in day-use areas

such as picnic areas, but are unrestricted on trails. Hunting is allowed in season.

Access and Fees

Parking and access are free. Trails are closed during the spring mud season, usually mid-April to mid-May. Route 108 is not maintained through Smuggler's Notch once the snow falls. But the road often has a packed-snow surface in winter, making it possible to drive up from the Jeffersonville side with a four-wheel-drive vehicle, or ski or hike up from either side.

Maps

The *Northern Vermont Hiking Trail Map,* which covers Mount Mansfield, Camel's Hump, Lake Willoughby, Cotton Brook, Little River, the Worcester Range, and Mount Elmore, is available from the Green Mountain Club for $4.95 for nonmembers; as is the waterproof End-to-End Map of the Long Trail, for $8.95. For a topographic area map, request Mount Mansfield from USGS Map Sales, Federal Center, Box 25286, Denver, CO 80225, 888/ASK-USGS (888/275-8747), website: http://mapping.usgs.gov.

Directions

Drive to the turnout immediately north of the height of land on Route 108 in Smuggler's Notch, south of Jeffersonville and north of Stowe.

Contact

Smuggler's Notch State Park, Box 7248, Mountain Road, Stowe, VT 05672, 802/253-4014 in summer, 802/479-4280 in winter, or 800/658-6934. Vermont Department of Forests, Parks, and Recreation, 103 South Main Street, Waterbury, VT 05671-0601, 802/241-3655, website: www.state.vt.us/anr/fpr. Green Mountain Club Inc., 4711 Waterbury-Stowe Road, Waterbury Center, VT 05677, 802/244-7037, website: www.greenmountainclub.org.

🛇 MOUNT MANSFIELD: SUNSET RIDGE AND LAURA COWLES TRAILS

in Underhill State Park and Mount Mansfield State Forest in Underhill Center

Total distance: 6.2 miles round-trip   **Hiking time:** 4.5 hours

Difficulty: 8   **Rating:** 10

This 6.2-mile loop hike up Vermont's highest peak ascends the spectacular Sunset Ridge, much of it above the trees, with long views and rugged terrain more reminiscent of Mount Washington or Katahdin than of most peaks here in the Green Mountains, few of which have alpine terrain. About half of the two-mile ridge ascent is over exposed ground. The sweeping views from the ridge to the south and north toward the Green Mountains—including the prominent summit of Camel's Hump to the south—and west toward Lake Champlain and the Adirondack Mountains are often accompanied by strong winds and harsh weather. Be prepared for wintry conditions any time of year. This hike passes over the Chin, Mansfield's true summit at 4,393 feet, with a 360-degree view encompassing the entire sweep of Vermont, as well as New Hampshire's White Mountains to the east. As with virtually any trail up Mansfield, this is a popular hike in summer and fall, and even attracts winter climbers (who should have the proper gear and skills). The trail gains about 2,100 feet in elevation from the state park to the summit. For more details, see the next listing.

From the parking lot at the ranger station, hike up the dirt CCC Road for about a mile; just beyond a sharp right bend in the road, the blue-blazed Sunset Ridge Trail, marked by a sign, enters the woods. Follow the trail over two wooden footbridges spanning brooks to a junction just 0.1 mile from the road with the Laura Cowles Trail, branching right; you will descend that trail. Continuing up the Sunset Ridge Trail, ascending moderately, you'll see the first views through breaks in the forest within 0.5 mile from the road. At 0.7 mile, turn left onto the Cantilever Rock Trail and follow it 0.1 mile to its namesake rock, a needle-like formation projecting horizontally about 40 feet from high up a cliff face. Backtrack to the Sunset Ridge Trail and continue climbing up through forest marked by occasional large boulders. About one mile from the road, the trail makes a short step up exposed rocks and emerges above tree line for the first broad views south and west.

The trail then follows the ridge upward, over rocky terrain where scrub spruce grow close to the ground in places, to a junction at about two miles with the Laura Cowles Trail, branching right—this hike's descent route. Continue another 0.2 mile up the Sunset Ridge Trail to its terminus at the Long Trail, on Mansfield's exposed summit ridge. Turn left (north) and follow the Long Trail 0.2 mile to the Chin. Backtrack on the Long Trail and Sunset Ridge Trail to the Laura Cowles Trail, and descend the Laura Cowles, reentering the woods within 0.5 mile of the Sunset Ridge Trail. The Cowles Trail drops steadily for another 0.9 mile to its lower junction with the Sunset Ridge Trail. Turn left and walk 0.1 mile back to the CCC Road.

User Groups

Hikers and dogs. Dogs must be leashed. No wheelchair facilities. This trail should not be attempted in winter except by hikers experienced in mountaineering and prepared for severe winter weather, and is not suitable for bikes, horses, or skis. Hunting is allowed in season.

Access and Fees

From Memorial Day to Columbus Day, an entrance fee of $2.50 per person age 14 and older, and $2 for children age 4 to 13, is collected at the ranger station. Once the snow falls, the CCC Road is maintained only to a point about a half mile before the start of this hike, where winter visitors can park. Camping is prohibited except at the Green Mountain Club cabins and shelters.

Maps

The waterproof *End-to-End Map of the Long Trail* is available for $8.95 from the Green Mountain Club, as is the *Northern Vermont Hiking Trail Map,* which covers Mount Mansfield, Camel's Hump, Lake Willoughby, Cotton Brook, Little River, the Worcester Range, and Mount Elmore, for $4.95. For a topographic area map, request Mount Mansfield from USGS Map

Sales, Federal Center, Box 25286, Denver, CO 80225, 888/ASK-USGS (888/275-8747), website: http://mapping.usgs.gov.

Directions

From Route 15 in Underhill Flats, drive east on the road to Underhill Center. In Underhill Center, three miles from Route 15, continue straight past the Underhill Country Store for one mile and turn right (at a sign for Underhill State Park) onto Mountain Road/TH2. Drive approximately two miles farther to a large parking lot at the ranger station.

Contact

Underhill State Park, P.O. Box 249, Underhill Center, VT 05490, 802/899-3022 in summer, 802/879-5674 in winter, or 800/252-2363. Vermont Department of Forests, Parks, and Recreation, Essex Junction District, 111 West Street, Essex Junction, VT 05452, 802/879-6565. Vermont Department of Forests, Parks, and Recreation Commissioner's Office, 103 South Main Street, Waterbury, VT 05671-0601, 802/241-3655, website: www.state.vt.us/anr/fpr. Green Mountain Club Inc., 4711 Waterbury-Stowe Road, Waterbury Center, VT 05677, 802/244-7037, website: www.greenmountainclub.org.

8 MOUNT MANSFIELD: THE HELL BROOK AND CLIFF TRAILS

in Smuggler's Notch State Park and Mount Mansfield State Forest in Stowe

Total distance: 5.8 miles round-trip

Hiking time: 6 hours

Difficulty: 9

Rating: 10

This is one of the hardest routes I've hiked in New England, linking some of the steepest, most rugged trails on Vermont's highest peak, Mount Mansfield. This 5.8-mile hike can take even fit hikers six hours to complete because of the scrambling involved on parts of it—and the potential for harsh weather. My wife and I did this hike with two friends in early September one year, and ran into freezing fog and rime ice at Mansfield's higher elevations. This hike ascends more than 2,500 feet in elevation. Most trail junctions are marked by signs, and the Long Trail is marked by white blazes.

From the Big Spring parking area, cross the road and walk uphill 150 feet to the Hell Brook Trail (there may be no sign). It climbs very steeply, through dense and often wet forest where you find yourself grabbing roots and tree branches for aid in places.

the author's wife on the Cliff Trail, Mount Mansfield

At 0.9 mile, the Hell Brook Cutoff branches left, but stay to the right on the Hell Brook Trail, at 1.3 miles reaching a junction with the Adam's Apple Trail on the left. The Bear Pond Trail heading north from this junction has been closed, although you may still be able to access scenic Lake of the Clouds on a short spur trail a very short distance down the former Bear Pond Trail. Climb the Adam's Apple Trail 0.1 mile to the rocky secondary summit of Mount Mansfield (known as the Adam's Apple) for excellent views of the true summit lying a stone's throw to the south. Descend over the Adam's Apple another 0.1 mile to rejoin the Hell Brook Trail and reach the Long Trail at Eagle Pass. Hikers looking to cut this loop short can descend the Long Trail by turning left and hiking for two miles to Route 108; once reaching the road, turn left and walk 0.5 mile to Big Spring.

This hike bears right at Eagle Pass onto the Long Trail southbound, climbing the steep cliffs of Mansfield's summit for 0.3 mile onto the Chin, Mansfield's true summit at 4,393 feet. The Green Mountains reach to the north and south horizons; to the west is Lake Champlain and New York's Adirondack Mountains, and to the east you can see New Hampshire's White Mountains on a clear day. The Long Trail continues south over Mansfield's long, exposed summit ridge, the most extensive of Vermont's few alpine areas, with fragile and rare vegetation; stay on the trail or walk on bare rock.

Stay on the Long Trail southbound along the ridge for 0.4 mile, then turn left onto the Cliff Trail. Within 0.1 mile, a spur trail leads right 50 feet to the Cave of the Winds, a deep joint in the cliff. Continue along the Cliff Trail, descending over very rocky terrain below the imposing cliffs of the summit ridge to your right, and overlooking Smuggler's Notch and the ski area below on your left. Three-tenths of a mile down the trail, a path to the left leads 0.1 mile downhill to the top of the ski area gondola; hikers uncomfortable with the difficulty of the Cliff Trail can bail out here and hike down a ski trail, bearing in mind that the Cliff Trail's greatest challenges lie ahead.

Continuing on the Cliff Trail, in another 0.1 mile you'll reach Wall Street, where the trail squeezes through a claustrophobia-inducing gap between towering rock walls. For the next 0.7 mile, the Cliff Trail climbs up and down over rock and through dense subalpine forest, leading hikers up wooden ladders bolted into sheer rock. At trail's end, turn left onto the summit road and follow it downhill for nearly a half mile, then turn left onto the Haselton Trail, which coincides here with a ski trail called Nose Dive. This descends at a steep grade that is hard on the knees. Watch for where the Haselton Trail reenters the woods, within 0.3 mile, on the left. It's two miles from the Cliff Trail to the ski area parking lot via the Haselton Trail.

User Groups

Hikers and dogs. Dogs must be leashed. No wheelchair facilities. This trail should not be attempted in winter except by hikers experienced in mountaineering and prepared for severe winter weather, and is not suitable for bikes, horses, or skis. Hunting is allowed in season.

Access and Fees

Parking and access are free. Route 108 is not maintained through Smuggler's Notch once the snow falls, only to a point about a mile east of this hike's start. Camping is prohibited except at the Green Mountain Club cabins and shelters. The Taft Lodge cabin is located on the Long Trail, 1.7 miles south of Route 108.

Maps

The waterproof *End-to-End Map of the Long Trail* is available for $8.95 from the Green Mountain Club, as is the *Northern Vermont Hiking Trail Map,* which covers Mount Mansfield, Camel's Hump, Lake Willoughby, Cotton Brook, Little River, the Worcester Range, and Mount Elmore, for $4.95. For a topographic area map, request Mount Mansfield from USGS Map Sales, Federal Center, Box 25286, Denver, CO 80225, 888/ASK-USGS (888/275-8747), website: http://mapping.usgs.gov.

Directions

You will need to either shuttle two vehicles for this hike or hike an extra 1.6 miles along Route 108 between the ski area and the Hell Brook Trailhead. Another option is to shorten this hike by descending the Long Trail, which would require walking 0.5 mile on Route 108 back to this hike's start. From the junction of Routes 108 and 100 in Stowe, drive 7.4 miles west on 108 and turn left into the gondola base station parking lot for the Mount Mansfield Ski Area; leave one vehicle there, turn back onto Route 108 west, and continue another 1.6 miles to the small dirt lot on the right at Big Spring, which is 1.2 miles east of the Route 108 height of land in Smuggler's Notch.

Contact

Vermont Department of Forests, Parks, and Recreation Region III-Northwest Vermont, 111 West Street, Essex Junction, VT 05452, 802/879-5666. Vermont Department of Forests, Parks, and Recreation Commissioner's Office, 103 South Main Street, Waterbury, VT 05671-0601, 802/241-3655, website: www.state .vt.us/anr/fpr. Green Mountain Club Inc., 4711 Waterbury-Stowe Road, Waterbury Center, VT 05677, 802/244-7037, website: www.greenmountainclub.org.

9 MOUNT MANSFIELD: THE LONG TRAIL

in Smuggler's Notch State Park in Stowe

Total distance: 4.6 miles round-trip   **Hiking time:** 3.5 hours

Difficulty: 8   **Rating:** 10

Probably the most commonly hiked route up Vermont's highest peak, 4,393-foot Mount Mansfield, the Long Trail is a good trail of only moderate difficulty. And just 2.3 miles from the road in Smuggler's Notch—after an elevation gain of nearly 2,800 feet—you are standing atop the Chin, Mansfield's true summit, with a 360-degree view taking in all of northern Vermont, including much of the Green Mountains, and stretching to New Hampshire's White Mountains, New York's Adirondacks, and Quebec. Predictably, this is a very popular hike that sees many boots on nice weekends in summer and fall. But I once hiked up this trail on a bone-chilling November day, had Taft Lodge all to myself for a night, and then saw no one as I bagged the summit the next morning.

taking pictures on the Long Trail, Mount Mansfield

Numerous features on Mansfield's long, completely exposed ridge bear names that derive from the mountain's resemblance, especially from the east, to a man's profile: the Chin, the Nose, the Forehead, the Upper and Lower Lip, and the Adam's Apple. Mansfield is one of just two peaks in Vermont—the other being Camel's Hump (see the three Camel's Hump listings in this chapter)—with a

COURTESY VERMONT DEPARTMENT OF TOURISM & MARKETING/ANDRE JENNY

significant alpine area, or area above the tree line. The rare plants that grow in this tundralike terrain are fragile, so take care to walk only on the trail or rocks. Be aware also that alpine terrain signals frequent harsh weather: Mansfield can attract wintry weather in any month of the year, so come here prepared for the worst and be willing to turn back whenever conditions turn threatening. A Green Mountain Club caretaker is on duty during the prime hiking season to assist hikers and ensure the protection of the alpine area. There are also TV and radio stations at the summit, a toll road up the mountain, and a ski area operating on its east side.

From the parking area, walk a short distance south on Route 108 and turn right (southbound) onto the white-blazed Long Trail. The trail climbs steadily, crossing a brook and changing direction a few times before reaching Taft Lodge at 1.7 miles. From the clearing at the lodge, you can see the imposing cliffs below the summit. Continue up the Long Trail. The trail emerges from the trees within 0.3 mile of the lodge and then climbs steeply another 0.3 mile to the summit. Return the way you came.

User Groups
Hikers and dogs. Dogs must be leashed. No wheelchair facilities. This trail should not be attempted in winter except by hikers experienced in mountaineering and prepared for severe winter weather, and is not suitable for bikes, horses, or skis. Hunting is allowed in season.

Access and Fees
Parking and access are free. Route 108 is not maintained through Smuggler's Notch once the snow falls, only to a point about a half mile east of this hike's start. Camping is prohibited except at the Green Mountain Club cabins and shelters. The Taft Lodge cabin is located on the Long Trail, 1.7 miles south of Route 108.

Maps
The waterproof *End-to-End Map of the Long Trail* is available for $8.95 from the Green Mountain Club, as is the *Northern Vermont Hiking Trail Map,* which covers Mount Mansfield, Camel's

Hump, Lake Willoughby, Cotton Brook, Little River, the Worcester Range, and Mount Elmore, for $4.95. For a topographic area map, request Mount Mansfield from USGS Map Sales, Federal Center, Box 25286, Denver, CO 80225, 888/ASK-USGS (888/275-8747), website: http://mapping.usgs.gov.

Directions

Drive to the roadside parking area immediately north of where the Long Trail northbound from Mount Mansfield reaches Route 108, 8.5 miles west of the junction of Routes 108 and 100 in Stowe, and 1.7 miles east of the height of land in Smuggler's Notch.

Contact

Smuggler's Notch State Park, Box 7248, Mountain Road, Stowe, VT 05672, 802/253-4014. Vermont Department of Forests, Parks, and Recreation Commissioner's Office, 103 South Main Street, Waterbury, VT 05671-0601, 802/241-3655, website: www.state.vt .us/anr/fpr. Green Mountain Club Inc., 4711 Waterbury-Stowe Road, Waterbury Center, VT 05677, 802/244-7037, website: www .greenmountainclub.org.

10 STOWE PINNACLE
in Putnam State Forest in Stowe

Total distance: 2.3 miles round-trip   **Hiking time:** 1.5 hours

Difficulty: 2   **Rating:** 10

This fairly easy round-trip hike of 2.3 miles leads to the open, craggy summit of Stowe Pinnacle, which is visible from the parking area. A great hike for young children—and quite popular with families—its summit offers excellent views, especially in a wide sweep from the northwest to the southwest, including Camel's Hump to the southwest, Mount Mansfield to the west, and the ski town of Stowe in the valley separating the pinnacle from Mansfield.

The trail begins at the rear of the parking area. Following easy terrain at first, the blue-blazed path traverses areas that are often muddy. It ascends moderately through the woods to a junction with the Skyline Trail (marked by a sign) just over a mile from the parking lot. Turn right and hike uphill another 0.1 mile to the Stowe Pinnacle summit. Return the way you came. See the special note in the Mount Hunger trail description (next listing) for a way to link the two hikes on a nice ridge walk.

User Groups
Hikers and snowshoers. No wheelchair facilities. This trail is not suitable for bikes, horses, or skis. Dogs are not allowed in day-use areas such as picnic areas, but are unrestricted on trails. Hunting is allowed in season.

Access and Fees
Parking and access are free. Trails are closed during the spring mud season, usually mid-April to mid-May.

Maps
The *Northern Vermont Hiking Trail Map,* which covers Mount Mansfield, Camel's Hump, Lake Willoughby (including Mounts Hor and Pisgah), Cotton Brook, Little River, the Worcester Range (including Stowe Pinnacle and Mount Hunger), and Mount Elmore, is available from the Green Mountain Club for $4.95. For a topographic area map, request Stowe from USGS

Map Sales, Federal Center, Box 25286, Denver, CO 80225, 888/ASK-USGS (888/275-8747), website: http://mapping.usgs.gov.

Directions

Take I-89 to Exit 10 and turn north onto Route 100. Continue about 10 miles and turn right onto School Street. Drive 0.3 mile and bear right onto Stowe Hollow Road. In another 1.5 miles, drive straight onto Upper Hollow Road and continue 0.7 mile to a parking area for the Pinnacle Trail on the left.

Contact

Vermont Department of Forests, Parks, and Recreation, Barre District, 324 North Main Street, Barre, VT 05641, 802/476-0170. Vermont Department of Forests, Parks, and Recreation Commissioner's Office, 103 South Main Street, Waterbury, VT 05671-0601, 802/241-3655, website: www.state.vt.us/anr/fpr. Green Mountain Club Inc., 4711 Waterbury-Stowe Road, Waterbury Center, VT 05677, 802/244-7037, website: www.greenmountain-club.org.

11 MOUNT HUNGER

in Putnam State Forest in Waterbury

Total distance: 4 miles round-trip   **Hiking time:** 3 hours

Difficulty: 8   **Rating:** 10

One of the nicest hikes in Vermont, yet requiring less effort than
higher Green Mountain peaks, Mount Hunger offers long views
in virtually every direction from its 3,539-foot summit of bare
rock. Dominating the western horizon is the long chain of the
Green Mountains, with Camel's Hump the prominent peak to the
southwest and Mount Mansfield, Vermont's highest, rising due
west. Between Hunger and Mansfield lies a pastoral valley of
open fields interspersed with sprawling forest. To the east, on a
clear day, you can make out the White Mountains, particularly
the towering wall of Franconia Ridge, and farther off, Mount
Washington. Hike up here in late fall or winter and you may see
the Whites capped in white. The ascent of Hunger is more than
2,200 feet. I hiked the longer loop described in the special note

below, over Hunger and
Stowe Pinnacle, with
two friends on a fall day
when the foliage was
near its peak, and we
enjoyed a colorful show.

From the parking lot,
the blue-blazed Water-
bury Trail makes a mod-
erately difficult ascent,
passing some cascades,
for nearly two miles be-
fore emerging above
tree line about 100
yards below the summit.
After reaching the sum-
mit, head back the way
you came.

Special note: A ridge
trail links the Mount

a hiker climbing Mount Hunger

Hunger summit with Stowe Pinnacle (see previous listing), and by shuttling cars to the parking lots at each trailhead, you can make this Worcester Range ridge walk of about seven miles (figure five hours). I recommend hiking up Mount Hunger and descending the Stowe Pinnacle end. From the Hunger summit, look for the cairns and blazes of the Skyline Trail heading north. The trail dips back into the woods and remains in the trees, but it's an interesting, if somewhat rugged, walk through a lush subalpine forest on a trail that experiences a fraction of the foot traffic seen on the primary trails up Hunger and Stowe Pinnacle. Some three miles or more from the top of Hunger, after the Skyline Trail passes over the wooded, 3,440-foot bump of Hogback Mountain, it descends, steeply in places, to a junction with the Pinnacle Trail. Bear left, reaching the top of Stowe Pinnacle in 0.1 mile. Descend the Pinnacle Trail 1.1 miles to the trailhead parking lot.

User Groups

Hikers and snowshoers. No wheelchair facilities. This trail is not suitable for bikes, horses, or skis. Dogs are not allowed in day-use areas such as picnic areas, but are unrestricted on trails. Hunting is allowed in season.

Access and Fees

Parking and access are free. Trails are closed during the spring mud season, usually mid-April to mid-May.

Maps

The *Northern Vermont Hiking Trail Map,* which covers Mount Mansfield, Camel's Hump, Lake Willoughby (including Mounts Hor and Pisgah), Cotton Brook, Little River, the Worcester Range (including Stowe Pinnacle and Mount Hunger), and Mount Elmore, is available from the Green Mountain Club for $4.95. For a topographic area map, request Stowe from USGS Map Sales, Federal Center, Box 25286, Denver, CO 80225, 888/ASK-USGS (888/275-8747), website: http://mapping.usgs.gov.

Directions

Take I-89 to Exit 10 and turn north onto Route 100. Drive about three miles and turn right onto Howard Avenue. Continue 0.4

12 MOUNT PHILO

in Mount Philo State Park between North Ferrisburg
and Charlotte

Total distance: 2.2 miles round-trip   **Hiking time:** 1.5 hours

Difficulty: 2   **Rating:** 9

The view from atop the cliffs of 968-foot Mount Philo far exceeds the expectations I had while driving toward this tiny hill. The bucolic Champlain Valley sprawls before you, flanked by the Green Mountains chain stretching far southward and the brooding Adirondack Mountains rising across Lake Champlain. This 2.2-mile loop over the summit is somewhat steep in places, although not difficult. When the road is open, you can drive to the top of Philo and walk about 0.1 mile to the cliff overlooks.

The blue-blazed trail begins just past the gate, on the left. The trail—which tends to be muddy and slippery in spring—winds up Mount Philo, crossing the summit road once, to the overlooks. After taking in the views, continue past the summit overlooks on a dirt road for 0.1 mile to a large parking lot and descend the paved park road 1.2 miles back to the hike's start.

User Groups

Hikers, snowshoers, and dogs. Dogs must be leashed. No wheelchair facilities. This trail is not suitable for bikes, horses, or skis; bike riders and skiers should take the summit road up and down.

Access and Fees

An entrance fee of $2.50 per person age 14 and older, and $2 for children age 4 to 13, is charged from Memorial Day through Columbus Day. Trails are closed during the spring mud season, usually mid-April to mid-May. The park road is not maintained in winter, making it a strenuous cross-country skiing route up the mountain.

Maps

While no map is necessary for this hike, a free, basic map is available at park entrances for virtually all state parks. For a topographic area map, request Mount Philo from USGS Map

Sales, Federal Center, Box 25286, Denver, CO 80225, 888/ASK-USGS (888/275-8747), website: http://mapping.usgs.gov.

Directions
From U.S. 7, about 1.2 miles north of North Ferrisburg and 2.5 miles south of the junction of U.S. 7 and Route F5 in Charlotte, turn east onto State Park Road. Drive 0.5 mile to a parking lot at the base of the mountain, just outside the gate.

Contact
Mount Philo State Park, 5425 Mount Philo Road, Charlotte, VT 05445; or RD 1 Box 1049, North Ferrisburgh, VT 05473, 802/425-2390 in summer, 802/483-2001 in winter. Vermont Department of Forests, Parks, and Recreation Commissioner's Office, 103 South Main Street, Waterbury, VT 05671-0601, 802/241-3655, website: www.state.vt.us/anr/fpr.

13 CAMEL'S HUMP: FOREST CITY/ BURROWS TRAILS LOOP

in Camel's Hump State Park in Huntington Center

Total distance: 6.4 miles round-trip   **Hiking time:** 4.5 hours

Difficulty: 8   **Rating:** 10

With the only undeveloped alpine area in the Green Mountain
State and a skyline that sets itself apart from everything else for
miles, 4,083-foot Camel's Hump may be Vermont's finest peak.
The views from its distinctive summit are among the best in New
England. To the west are the Adirondacks and Lake Champlain;
the Green Mountains stretch out in a long chain to the south; to
the southeast rises the prominent mound of Mount Ascutney; to
the northeast lie Mount Hunger and Stowe Pinnacle in the
Worcester Range; far to the northeast, on a clear day, the White
Mountains are visible; and to the north, when not smothered in
clouds, are Bolton Mountain and Mount Mansfield.

Camel's Hump is one of the state's most popular peaks, too,
attracting hundreds of hikers on nice weekend days in summer
and fall. But twice I've had the summit all to myself, simply by
hiking at times when other people don't hike. On one sunny,
but bitterly cold, early spring afternoon (before mud season), I
gazed through thin haze at the white caps of New Hampshire's
Presidential Range and Franconia Ridge, seeming to float in
the sky. The treeless summit of Camel's Hump hosts one of the
state's few alpine vegetation zones, plants threatened by heavy
hiker use. Help protect them by walking only on the trail or
bare rock.

You can hike this loop in either direction, but I recommend
going from Forest City to the Long Trail and down the Burrows
because the exposed ascent of the Long Trail up Camel's
Hump's southern ridge is a wonderful climb that builds excite-
ment for the summit. (For a shorter hike, the Burrows round-trip
to the summit is 5.4 miles.) The vertical ascent on the loop is
about 2,700 feet. The Forest City and Burrows Trails are well-
worn paths and well marked with blue blazes; the Long Trail is
blazed white. Trail junctions have been marked with signs in the
past, but don't count on them. From the Burrows Trailhead, turn

right onto the connector trail leading 0.1 mile to the Forest City Trail and then turn left onto it, hiking east. The trail ascends at a moderate grade, reaching the Long Trail about 1.6 miles from the Burrows Trailhead. Turn left (north) on the Long Trail and follow it for nearly two miles to the summit, climbing below and around spectacular cliffs. Beyond the summit, stay on the Long Trail for another 0.3 mile to the Camel's Hump hut clearing and then turn left (west) on the Burrows Trail, which leads 2.4 miles back to the trailhead.

User Groups

Hikers and dogs. Dogs must be leashed above tree line. No wheelchair facilities. This trail should not be attempted in winter except by hikers experienced in mountaineering and prepared for severe winter weather, and is not suitable for bikes, horses, or skis. Hunting is allowed in season.

Access and Fees

Parking and access are free. The trails are closed to hiking during mud season, mid-April to Memorial Day. Camping is prohibited except at the two Green Mountain Club cabins—Montclair Glen Lodge, near the Burrows and Long Trails junction, and Bamforth Ridge shelter 5.4 miles north of Montclair Glen Lodge on the Long Trail—and at the Hump Brook tenting area, just off the Dean Trail. From Memorial Day weekend to Columbus Day, a Green Mountain Club caretaker is on duty and a $6-per-person nightly fee is collected to stay at either cabin.

Maps

A basic trail map with state park information is sometimes available at the trailhead hiker register. The *Northern Vermont Hiking Trail Map,* which covers Mount Mansfield, Camel's Hump, Lake Willoughby (including Mounts Hor and Pisgah), Cotton Brook, Little River, the Worcester Range (including Stowe Pinnacle and Mount Hunger), and Mount Elmore, is available from the Green Mountain Club and costs $4.95. For topographic area maps, request Huntington and Waterbury from USGS Map Sales, Federal Center, Box 25286, Denver, CO 80225, 888/ASK-USGS (888/275-8747), website: http://mapping.usgs.gov.

Directions

In Huntington Center, 2.5 miles south of the post office in Huntington Village, turn onto Camel's Hump Road at signs for Camel's Hump State Park. Follow the dirt road, bearing right at forks (state park signs point the way). At 2.8 miles from Huntington Center, there is a small parking area on the right at the Forest City Trailhead; you can start this loop from there (adding 1.5 miles to this hike's distance), or continue up the road another 0.7 mile to a larger parking area at the Burrows Trailhead.

Contact

Vermont Department of Forests, Parks, and Recreation Region III-Northwest Vermont, 111 West Street, Essex Junction, VT 05452, 802/879-5666. Vermont Department of Forests, Parks, and Recreation Commissioner's Office, 103 South Main Street, Waterbury, VT 05671-0601, 802/241-3655, website: www.state.vt.us/anr/fpr. Green Mountain Club Inc., 4711 Waterbury-Stowe Road, Waterbury Center, VT 05677, 802/244-7037, website: www.greenmountainclub.org.

14 CAMEL'S HUMP: LONG TRAIL/ BAMFORTH RIDGE

in Camel's Hump State Park in North Duxbury

Total distance: 11.8 miles round-trip   **Hiking time:** 8 hours

Difficulty: 9   **Rating:** 10

See the Camel's Hump: Forest City/Burrows Trails Loop (previous listing) for more descriptive information about Camel's Hump. The Long Trail from the north constitutes the most arduous route to the 4,083-foot Camel's Hump summit: 11.8 miles round-trip and some 3,700 feet of ascent. The Long Trail was relocated in 1996 onto this route, also known as the Bamforth Ridge Trail. (The former route of the Long Trail, which passed the Honey Hollow tenting area, has been closed, as has the tenting area.) The Long Trail ascends the rugged Bamforth Ridge, dipping and climbing repeatedly and often steeply, and traversing some boggy terrain. But open ledges at many points along the ridge offer the most sustained views of any routes up Camel's Hump.

From the parking lot, follow the Long Trail's white blazes south. The trail climbs steadily to Camel's Hump clearing at 5.6 miles. From the clearing, the trail grows fairly steep and rugged to the summit, 5.9 miles from the road. Return the way you came.

view from the Long Trail on Camel's Hump

User Groups

Hikers and dogs. Dogs must be leashed above tree line. No wheelchair facilities. This trail should not be attempted in winter except by hikers experienced in mountaineering and prepared for severe winter weather, and is not suitable for bikes, horses, or skis. Hunting is allowed in season.

Access and Fees

Parking and access are free. The trails are closed to hiking during mud season, roughly mid-April to Memorial Day. Camping is prohibited except at the two Green Mountain Club cabins—Montclair Glen Lodge, near the Burrows and Long Trails junction, and Bamforth Ridge shelter 5.4 miles north of Montclair Glen Lodge on the Long Trail—and at the Hump Brook tenting area, just off the Dean Trail. From Memorial Day weekend to Columbus Day, a Green Mountain Club caretaker is on duty and a $6-per-person nightly fee is collected to stay at the two cabins.

Maps

A basic trail map with state park information is sometimes available at the trailhead hiker register. The waterproof *End-to-End Map of the Long Trail* is available for $8.95 from the Green Mountain Club, as is the *Northern Vermont Hiking Trail Map*, which covers Mount Mansfield, Camel's Hump, Lake Willoughby, Cotton Brook, Little River, the Worcester Range, and Mount Elmore, for $4.95. For topographic area maps, request Huntington and Waterbury from USGS Map Sales, Federal Center, Box 25286, Denver, CO 80225, 888/ASK-USGS (888/275-8747), website: http://mapping.usgs.gov.

Directions

From the south, take I-89 to Exit 10. Turn south, drive about a half mile to the end of the road, and turn left onto U.S. 2 east. Continue 1.3 miles and then turn right onto Route 100 south. Proceed just 0.2 mile and turn right at a sign for the Duxbury Elementary School. Just 0.2 mile farther, bear right onto a dirt road at a sign for Camel's Hump. Five miles down that road, continue straight ahead at a sign directing you left for Camel's

Hump trails. The parking lot for the Long Trail/Bamforth Ridge Trail lies 2.7 miles farther down the road.

From the north, take I-89 to Exit 11 for U.S. 2 east. Drive about five miles into Jonesville, and just beyond the post office (on the left), turn right, crossing the bridge over the Winooski River. At 0.2 mile from U.S. 2, turn left onto Duxbury Road and continue 3.3 miles to the Long Trail/Bamforth Ridge Trail parking area on the right.

Contact

Vermont Department of Forests, Parks, and Recreation Region III-Northwest Vermont, 111 West Street, Essex Junction, VT 05452, 802/879-5666. Vermont Department of Forests, Parks, and Recreation Commissioner's Office, 103 South Main Street, Waterbury, VT 05671-0601, 802/241-3655, website: www.state.vt.us/anr/fpr. Green Mountain Club Inc., 4711 Waterbury-Stowe Road, Waterbury Center, VT 05677, 802/244-7037, website: www.greenmountainclub.org.

15 CAMEL'S HUMP: MONROE/ ALPINE TRAILS LOOP

in Camel's Hump State Park in North Duxbury

Total distance: 6.6 miles round-trip   **Hiking time:** 4.5 hours

Difficulty: 8   **Rating:** 10

The Monroe Trail—renamed for Professor Will Monroe, father of the Monroe Skyline (see listing in this chapter)—may be the most popular route up a very popular mountain. For more descriptive information about Camel's Hump, see the Camel's Hump: Forest City/Burrows Trails Loop in this chapter.

This 6.6-mile loop, which ascends about 2,600 feet, includes an interesting variation from the Monroe Trail onto the Alpine Trail. From the parking lot, the blue-blazed Monroe Trail ascends at a moderate grade at first but grows steeper as you climb higher. Trail sections are often wet, even into autumn. At 2.5 miles, turn left onto the yellow-blazed Alpine Trail, which is wooded and fairly rugged along this stretch. Within 0.5 mile, you pass near the wing of a WWII bomber that crashed into the mountain during a wartime training flight at night.

Just beyond the wreckage, the Alpine Trail meets the Long Trail; turn right (north) on the white-blazed Long Trail, quickly emerging from the trees for your first sweeping views from below the towering cliffs on the Camel's Hump south face. The Long Trail swings left below the cliffs and ascends the mountain's west face to its open, 4,083-foot summit, 0.2 mile from the Alpine Trail. Continue on the Long Trail north over the summit, descending rocky terrain for 0.3 mile to the Camel's Hump hut clearing. Turn right onto the Monroe Trail, which takes you down 3.1 miles to the parking area.

User Groups

Hikers and dogs. Dogs must be leashed above tree line. No wheelchair facilities. This trail should not be attempted in winter except by hikers experienced in mountaineering and prepared for severe winter weather and is not suitable for bikes, horses, or skis. Hunting is allowed in season.

Access and Fees

Parking and access are free. The trails are closed to hiking during mud season, roughly mid-April to Memorial Day. Winter parking is in the lot for Camel's Hump View, 0.5 mile before the Couching Lion site. Camping is prohibited except at the two Green Mountain Club cabins—Montclair Glen Lodge, near the Burrows and Long Trails junction, and Bamforth Ridge shelter 5.4 miles north of Montclair Glen Lodge on the Long Trail—and at the Hump Brook tenting area, just off the Dean Trail. From Memorial Day weekend to Columbus Day, a Green Mountain Club caretaker is on duty and a $6-per-person nightly fee is collected to stay at either cabin.

Maps

A basic trail map with state park information is sometimes available at the trailhead hiker register. The waterproof *End-to-End Map of the Long Trail* is available for $8.95 from the Green Mountain Club, as is the *Northern Vermont Hiking Trail Map,* which covers Mount Mansfield, Camel's Hump, Lake Willoughby, Cotton Brook, Little River, the Worcester Range, and Mount Elmore, for $4.95. For topographic area maps, request Huntington and Waterbury from USGS Map Sales, Federal Center, Box 25286, Denver, CO 80225, 888/ASK-USGS (888/275-8747), website: http://mapping.usgs.gov.

Directions

From the south, take I-89 to Exit 10. Turn south, drive about a half mile to the end of the road, and turn left onto U.S. 2 east. Continue 1.3 miles and then turn right onto Route 100 south. Proceed just 0.2 mile and turn right onto Duxbury Road; continue six miles down that road, then turn left at a sign for Camel's Hump trails. Drive 1.2 miles and bear left over a bridge. Continue another 2.4 miles to the parking lot at the end of the road, at the so-called Couching Lion site.

From the north, take I-89 to Exit 11 for U.S. 2 east. Drive about five miles into Jonesville, and just beyond the post office (on the left), turn right, crossing the bridge over the Winooski River. In 0.2 mile, turn left onto Duxbury Road and continue six miles to the sign for Camel's Hump trails. Turn right, cross the bridge at 1.2 miles, and continue 2.4 miles to the Couching Lion site.

Contact

Vermont Department of Forests, Parks, and Recreation Region III-Northwest Vermont, 111 West Street, Essex Junction, VT 05452, 802/879-5666. Vermont Department of Forests, Parks, and Recreation Commissioner's Office, 103 South Main Street, Waterbury, VT 05671-0601, 802/241-3655, website: www.state.vt.us/anr/fpr. Green Mountain Club Inc., 4711 Waterbury-Stowe Road, Waterbury Center, VT 05677, 802/244-7037, website: www.greenmountainclub.org.

16 CAMEL'S HUMP VIEW

in Camel's Hump State Park in North Duxbury

Total distance: 0.2 miles round-trip   **Hiking time:** 0.25 hour

Difficulty: 1   **Rating:** 7

Here is an easy walk of just 0.2 mile round-trip to a striking view of Camel's Hump for folks not inclined to actually climb the mountain. It's also a pleasant trail for hikers or cross-country skiers looking for an unusual angle on arguably Vermont's most recognizable peak. From the parking lot, walk up the left fork of the Camel's Hump View Trail, crossing over Sinnott Brook on a wooden bridge and reaching a wooden bench on the right at 0.1 mile. From the bench, look across a clearing for a view of Camel's Hump. You can turn back from here or continue up the trail for a 0.5-mile loop back to the parking lot. The Ridley Crossing ski trail diverges off this loop about halfway through it, leading to the Beaver Meadow Trail, where you would turn right to loop back to the main road just below the Couching Lion site.

User Groups

Hikers, dogs, skiers, snowshoers, and wheelchair users. Dogs must be leashed. This trail is not suitable for bikes or horses. Hunting is allowed in season.

Access and Fees

Parking and access are free. The trails in the park are closed to hiking during mud season, roughly mid-April to Memorial Day.

Maps

No map is necessary for this hike, although a basic trail map of Camel's Hump State Park is available at the trailhead hiker register at the Couching Lion site. For topographic area maps, request Huntington and Waterbury from USGS Map Sales, Federal Center, Box 25286, Denver, CO 80225, 888/ASK-USGS (888/275-8747), website: http://mapping.usgs.gov.

Directions

From the south, take I-89 to Exit 10. Turn south, drive about a half mile to the end of the road, and turn left onto U.S. 2 east. Continue 1.3 miles and then turn right onto Route 100 south. Proceed just 0.2 mile and turn right onto Duxbury Road; continue six miles down that road, then turn left at a sign for Camel's Hump trails. Drive 1.2 miles and bear left over a bridge. Continue another 1.9 miles, turn left (0.5 mile before the Couching Lion site), and drive another 0.2 mile to the Lewis Place parking area.

From the north, take I-89 to Exit 11 for U.S. 2 east. Drive about five miles into Jonesville, and just beyond the post office (on the left), turn right, crossing the bridge over the Winooski River. In 0.2 mile turn left onto Duxbury Road and continue six miles to the sign for Camel's Hump trails. Turn right, cross the bridge at 1.2 miles, and 1.9 miles past the bridge turn left for the Lewis Place parking area.

Contact

Vermont Department of Forests, Parks, and Recreation Commissioner's Office, 103 South Main Street, Waterbury, VT 05671-0601, 802/241-3655, website: www.state.vt.us/anr/fpr.

17 BIG DEER MOUNTAIN
in Groton State Forest

Total distance: 4.2 miles round-trip   **Hiking time:** 3 hours

Difficulty: 4   **Rating:** 8

I first discovered Groton State Forest, in Vermont's Northeast Kingdom, while on a bike tour several years ago; that time, I only spent a night in the campground. More recently, I returned with a friend to mountain bike its forest roads and hike up Big Deer Mountain, which has good views for a hill not even 2,000 feet high. This hike begins from different parking areas, depending upon whether the road into the New Discovery Campground is open. The elevation gained is about 300 feet.

In winter, parking at the gate, walk 0.1 mile past the gate to a field; in summer, backtrack the road from the Osmore Pond picnic area to the field. Facing that field (as you would in winter, walking from the gate), turn left onto an obvious dirt forest road and follow it 0.3 mile and turn right onto the Big Deer Mountain Trail (marked by a sign). Follow the blue blazes through the woods on a trail that's mostly flat for 1.1 miles. Then, at a trail junction, continue straight ahead, climbing about 200 feet in elevation over 0.6 mile of rocky trail onto Big Deer Mountain. The trail ends at open ledges with a view to the south, overlooking Lake Groton. Just before the trail's end, a side path leads left a short distance to another open ledge with a view east from high above Peacham Bog. On a clear day, you can see the White Mountains. Backtrack 0.6 mile to the junction and turn left onto the Big Deer Mountain Trail toward Osmore Pond. It descends gently, crosses a marshy area, passes over a slight rise, and then descends more steeply to a trail junction near the south end of Osmore Pond, 0.9 mile from the last junction. Turn right onto the Osmore Pond Hiking Loop, a rock-strewn but flat trail that parallels the pond's east shore and loops around its north end. In winter, about 0.7 mile from the trail junction at the pond's south end, turn right again onto a connector trail leading back to the New Discovery Campground. In summer, follow the loop trail around the pond to the picnic area.

User Groups

Hikers and snowshoers. No wheelchair facilities. This trail is not suitable for bikes, horses, or skis. Dogs are not allowed in day-use areas such as picnic areas, but are unrestricted on trails. Hunting is allowed in season.

Access and Fees

An entrance fee of $2.50 per person age 14 and older, and $2 for children age 4 to 13, is charged from a week before Memorial Day to Labor Day. Trails are closed during the spring mud season, usually mid-April to mid-May. The road into the New Discovery Campground is closed and blocked by a gate when the park is closed, from Labor Day to Memorial Day weekend.

Maps

A free, basic map is available at park entrances for virtually all state parks. For a topographic area map, request Marshfield from USGS Map Sales, Federal Center, Box 25286, Denver, CO 80225, 888/ASK-USGS (888/275-8747), website: http://mapping.usgs.gov.

Directions

From I-91, take Exit 17 onto U.S. 302 west. Drive about 8.8 miles and turn right onto Route 232 north. Drive 9.4 miles and turn right into the New Discovery Campground. From Memorial Day weekend to Labor Day, continue 0.1 mile past the open gate to a field, turn right, and drive to the picnic shelter on Osmore Pond to park. In winter, park at the gate without blocking it.

Contact

New Discovery Campground, 802/426-3042. Vermont Department of Forests, Parks, and Recreation Commissioner's Office, 103 South Main Street, Waterbury, VT 05671-0601, 802/241-3655, website: www.state.vt.us/anr/fpr.

18 KINGSLAND BAY STATE PARK

in Ferrisburg

Total distance: 1 mile round-trip   **Hiking time:** 0.75 hour

Difficulty: 1   **Rating:** 7

An unmarked but obvious trail begins behind the tennis courts and soon forks, creating a loop through the conifer woods on a point that juts into Lake Champlain; the loop can be done in either direction. Much of the one-mile, easy trail remains in the woods, with limited lake views; there is one clearing with a view northeast toward Camel's Hump and the Green Mountains.

User Groups

Hikers and snowshoers. No wheelchair facilities. This trail is not suitable for bikes, horses, or skis. Dogs are not allowed in day-use areas such as picnic areas, but are unrestricted on trails. Hunting is allowed in season.

Access and Fees

An entrance fee of $2.50 is charged for persons 14 and older, and $2 for children age 4 to 13, from a week before Memorial Day to Labor Day. Trails are closed during the spring mud season, usually mid-April to mid-May. The park road is closed to traffic in the off-season, but you can walk the road, adding a mile round-trip to this hike's distance.

Maps

While no map is necessary for this hike, a free, basic map is available at park entrances for virtually all state parks. For a topographic area map, request Westport from USGS Map Sales, Federal Center, Box 25286, Denver, CO 80225, 888/ASK-USGS (888/275-8747), website: http://mapping.usgs.gov.

Directions

From the junction of U.S. 7 and Route 22A north of Vergennes, drive north on U.S. 7 for 0.5 mile and then turn left (west) onto Tuppers Crossing Road. Proceed 0.4 mile and bear right onto Bottsford Road. Drive 0.8 mile and continue straight through a crossroads onto Hawkins Road. Or from North Ferrisburg, drive south on U.S. 7 for about four miles and turn right (west) onto Little Chicago Road. Continue a mile and turn right onto Hawkins. Follow Hawkins Road for 3.4 miles and then turn right at a sign into Kingsland Bay State Park. Follow the dirt park road about a half mile and park at the roadside near the tennis courts.

Contact

Kingsland Bay State Park, RR 1, Box 245, 787 Kingsland Bay State Park Road, Ferrisburg, VT 05456, 802/877-3445 in summer, 802/483-2001 in winter, or 800/658-1622. Vermont Department of Forests, Parks, and Recreation Commissioner's Office, 103 South Main Street, Waterbury, VT 05671-0601, 802/241-3655, website: www.state.vt.us/anr/fpr.

19 BUTTON BAY STATE PARK
in Ferrisburg

Total distance: 1 mile round-trip **Hiking time:** 0.75 hour

Difficulty: 1 **Rating:** 8

The park, named for the buttonlike concretions formed by clay deposits found along the shore, has been visited by such famous persons as Samuel De Champlain (in 1609), Ethan Allen (in 1776), Ben Franklin (also in 1776), and Benedict Arnold (in 1777). This flat walk of a mile round-trip along a wide gravel road leads to Button Point, where the land thrusts a finger of rocks into Lake Champlain and the views encompass a wide sweep from Camel's Hump and the Green Mountains to the east, to the Adirondacks across the lake. From the parking lots, walk the gravel road 0.5 mile to its end at Button Point. Return the same way.

User Groups
Hikers, bikers, skiers, and snowshoers. Wheelchair users can drive the dirt road beyond the public parking lots to wheelchair-accessible parking just 100 yards before the point on Lake Champlain. This trail is not suitable for horses. Dogs are not allowed in day-use areas such as picnic areas, but are unrestricted on trails. Hunting is allowed in season.

Access and Fees
An entrance fee of $2.50 per person age 14 and older, and $2 for children age 4 to 13, is charged from Memorial Day to Columbus Day. Trails are closed during the spring mud season, usually mid-April to Memorial Day. The park road is closed to traffic in the off-season, but you can walk the road, adding a mile round-trip to this hike's distance.

Maps
While no map is necessary for this hike, a free, basic map is available to virtually all state parks. For a topographic area map, request Westport from USGS Map Sales, Federal Center, Box 25286, Denver, CO 80225, 888/ASK-USGS (888/275-8747), website: http://mapping.usgs.gov.

Directions

From the green in the center of Vergennes, drive south on Route 22A for 0.5 mile and turn right onto Panton Road. Proceed 1.4 miles and turn right onto Basin Harbor Road. Continue 4.5 miles, turn left onto Button Bay Road, and follow it 0.6 mile to the entrance on the right to Button Bay State Park. Drive about a half mile down the park road to two gravel parking lots on the left, across from the pavilion.

Contact

Button Bay State Park, RD 3, Box 4075, 5 Button Bay State Park Road, Vergennes, VT 05491, 802/475-2377 in summer, 802/483-2001 in winter, or 800/658-1622. Vermont Department of Forests, Parks, and Recreation Commissioner's Office, 103 South Main Street, Waterbury, VT 05671-0601, 802/241-3655, website: www.state.vt.us/anr/fpr.

20 THE LONG TRAIL: ROUTE 17, APPALACHIAN GAP, TO THE WINOOSKI RIVER

between Appalachian Gap and North Duxbury

Total distance: 18.4 miles one-way   **Hiking time:** 2–3 days

Difficulty: 8   **Rating:** 10

This 18.4-mile leg of the Long Trail is arguably its most spectacular stretch. The hike's centerpiece is 4,083-foot Camel's Hump, but less well-known Burnt Rock Mountain offers one of the best views on the Long Trail; Molly Stark's Balcony is another choice spot, and the trail harbors some gems in the woods like Ladder Ravine. This is the northern section of the fabled Monroe Skyline (see listing in this chapter). The one-way traverse covers rugged terrain and involves more than 3,500 feet of climbing and much more descending (the descent from the summit of Camel's Hump to the Winooski River alone is about 3,700 feet); it can easily take three days.

This hike, especially the Camel's Hump area, is popular in summer and fall, and the shelters tend to fill up quickly on weekends. When above tree line, remember that the fragile alpine vegetation suffers under boots, so stay on the marked trail or rocks. Also be advised that water sources are few along the ridge and generally found only at the shelters.

From Route 17, the Long Trail northbound climbs steeply out of Appalachian Gap for 0.4 mile, descends steeply, and then climbs again to the top of Molly Stark Mountain at one mile from the road. At 1.3 miles, the trail passes over Molly Stark's Balcony, a rock outcropping atop a cliff rising above the trees, where you get a long view north toward Camel's Hump and northeast to the Worcester Range, which includes Mount Hunger and Stowe Pinnacle. Descending more easily, the Long Trail reaches the Beane Trail at 2.6 miles, which leads left (west) about 100 feet to the Birch Glen Camp, and 0.9 mile to a road that travels 1.5 miles to Hanksville. The Long Trail follows easier ground from here, ascending gradually to Cowles Cove shelter at 5.5 miles. Climbing slightly, the trail passes the Hedgehog Brook

Trail at 6.4 miles, which descends right (east) 2.5 miles to a road two miles outside North Fayston. Then the Long Trail quickly grows more rugged, climbing to the open, rocky Burnt Rock Mountain summit seven miles into this hike. At 3,168 feet, the summit should be wooded, but it was denuded by fires years ago, and today offers long views of the Green Mountains arcing southward, the Worcester Range to the east and the White Mountains beyond, the Lake Champlain southern tip to the southwest, and New York's Adirondacks brooding darkly behind the lake.

Follow the blazes and cairns carefully as the trail makes numerous turns over Burnt Rock's bare crown. The Long Trail reenters the lush, wild forest, reaching Ladder Ravine at 7.4 miles, a perpetually wet place where a wooden ladder is employed to descend a short cliff. Continuing over rough terrain, the trail climbs over the wooded humps of Ira Allen (at 8.5 miles) and Ethan Allen's two peaks (at 9.5 and 9.6 miles) and then descends past the Allis Trail at 10.4 miles; that trail leads straight ahead to Allis Lookout, where there is a view of the mountains to the north, and terminates at the Long Trail in 0.3 mile. The Long Trail, meanwhile, swings left and descends to Montclair Glen Lodge at 10.6 miles. Just downhill from the cabin on the Long Trail, the Forest City Trail departs left (west), dropping gradually for 2.2 miles to a road outside Huntington Center (see Camel's Hump: Forest City/Burrows Trails Loop, this chapter).

The Long Trail then begins the ascent of Camel's Hump, passing the Dean Trail in Wind Gap (at 10.8 miles), which leads right (east) 2.3 miles to the Couching Lion site. Traversing open ledges on the east side of the Hump's southern ridge, the Long Trail affords excellent views south along the Green Mountains and east in a wide sweep from Mount Ascutney to the Worcester Range. It then reenters the woods again briefly, climbing steeply to a junction at 12.3 miles with the Alpine Trail, which departs right (east) and provides an alternate route around the summit in bad weather, swinging north and reaching the Bamforth Ridge Trail/Long Trail in 1.7 miles. There is 0.2 mile more of steep, exposed hiking, with the trail swinging left around tall cliffs and ascending the west face up the rocky summit cone of Camel's Hump.

Dropping north off the summit, the Long Trail reaches the Camel's Hump hut clearing at 12.8 miles, where the Monroe Trail leaves right (east), descending 3.1 miles to the Couching Lion site, and the Burrows Trail leaves left (west), descending 2.6 miles to a road outside Huntington Center. Reentering the woods, the Long Trail—since being re-routed in 1996—follows the old Bamforth Ridge Trail north. The descent is rugged, dipping and climbing repeatedly and often steeply, and traversing some boggy terrain. But open ledges at many points along the ridge offer the best views of any trail on Camel's Hump. The Long Trail reaches the parking lot on River Road at 18.4 miles.

User Groups

Hikers and dogs. Dogs must be leashed above tree line. No wheelchair facilities. This trail should not be attempted in winter except by hikers experienced in mountaineering and prepared for severe winter weather, and is not suitable for bikes, horses, or skis. Hunting is allowed in season.

Access and Fees

Parking and access are free. The Long Trail is closed from Appalachian Gap to the Winooski River from mid-April to Memorial Day. Much of this Long Trail section is in Camel's Hump State Park; the remainder is on private land. Camping is prohibited except at the Green Mountain Club shelters and campsites: the Birch Glen Camp, 2.6 miles north of Route 17 and 100 feet off the Long Trail on the Beane Trail; the Cowles Cove shelter, 5.5 miles north of Route 17; the Montclair Glen Lodge near the Forest City and Long Trails junction, 10.6 miles north of Route 17; and the Bamforth Ridge shelter 16 miles north of Route 17. From Memorial Day weekend to Columbus Day, a Green Mountain Club caretaker is on duty and a $6-per-person nightly fee is collected to stay at a cabin.

Maps

A basic trail map is available at trailheads in Camel's Hump State Park. The waterproof *End-to-End Map of the Long Trail* is available for $8.95 from the Green Mountain Club, as is the *Northern Vermont Hiking Trail Map,* which covers Mount Mansfield, Camel's Hump, Lake Willoughby, Cotton Brook, Little River, the Worcester Range, and Mount Elmore, for $4.95. For topographic area maps, request Mount Ellen, Huntington, and Waterbury from USGS Map Sales, Federal Center, Box 25286, Denver, CO 80225, 888/ASK-USGS (888/275-8747), website: http://mapping.usgs.gov.

Directions
You need to shuttle two vehicles for this one-way traverse. To hike south to north, as described here, leave one vehicle in the trailhead parking lot on River Road in North Duxbury (see Directions for Camel's Hump: Long Trail/Bamforth Ridge). Then drive to where the Long Trail crosses Route 17 in Appalachian Gap, three miles east of the Huntington Road and six miles west of Route 100 in Irasville.

Contact
Vermont Department of Forests, Parks, and Recreation Commissioner's Office, 103 South Main Street, Waterbury, VT 05671-0601, 802/241-3655, website: www.state.vt.us/anr/fpr. Green Mountain Club Inc., 4711 Waterbury-Stowe Road, Waterbury Center, VT 05677, 802/244-7037, website: www.greenmountainclub.org.

21 MOLLY STARK'S BALCONY
north of Appalachian Gap

Total distance: 2.6 miles round-trip

Hiking time: 2 hours

Difficulty: 6

Rating: 8

From Molly Stark's Balcony, a rocky ledge atop a cliff jutting above the woods, you get a long view north toward Camel's Hump and northeast to the Worcester Range, which includes Mount Hunger and Stowe Pinnacle. Though just a 2.6-mile round-trip climbing several hundred feet, this hike has very steep uphill stretches and descents. The Long Trail northbound climbs steeply out of Appalachian Gap for 0.4 mile, drops steeply, then climbs again to Molly Stark Mountain's highest point at one mile from the road. Continue north on the Long Trail for 0.3 mile to the balcony, a small ledge on the right side of the trail immediately before another steep downhill. Return the way you came.

User Groups
Hikers, snowshoers, and dogs. Dogs must be leashed. No wheelchair facilities. This trail is not suitable for bikes, horses, or skis. Hunting is allowed in season.

Access and Fees
Parking and access are free. The Long Trail is closed from Appalachian Gap to the Winooski River from mid-April to Memorial Day. This stretch of the Long Trail passes through Camel's Hump State Park, and camping is prohibited except at the Green Mountain Club shelters. The Birch Glen Camp is 1.3 miles north of Molly Stark's Balcony and 100 feet off the Long Trail on the Beane Trail.

Maps
The waterproof *End-to-End Map of the Long Trail* is available for $8.95 from the Green Mountain Club, as is the *Northern Vermont Hiking Trail Map,* which covers Mount Mansfield, Camel's Hump, Lake Willoughby, Cotton Brook, Little River, the Worcester Range, and Mount Elmore, for $4.95. For a topographic area map, request Mount Ellen from USGS Map

Sales, Federal Center, Box 25286, Denver, CO 80225, 888/ASK-USGS (888/275-8747), website: http://mapping.usgs.gov.

Directions
Drive to where the Long Trail crosses Route 17 in Appalachian Gap, three miles east of the Huntington Road and six miles west of Route 100 in Irasville.

Contact
Vermont Department of Forests, Parks, and Recreation Commissioner's Office, 103 South Main Street, Waterbury, VT 05671-0601, 802/241-3655, website: www.state.vt.us/anr/fpr. Green Mountain Club Inc., 4711 Waterbury-Stowe Road, Waterbury Center, VT 05677, 802/244-7037, website: www.greenmountainclub.org.

22 THE MONROE SKYLINE
between Middlebury Gap and North Duxbury

Total distance: 47.4 miles one-way **Hiking time:** 5–6 days

Difficulty: 8 **Rating:** 10

When the nation's first long-distance hiking trail was in its formative years, this stretch of nearly 50 miles was not along the high mountain ridges it now traverses. It was mired down in the woods, where the state forestry officials who did much of the early trail work wanted it to be so they could access forest fires. Then along came Professor Will Monroe, a respected botanist and author, who over several years beginning in 1916 became the catalyst behind the Green Mountain Club's effort to move the Long Trail up onto the rugged chain of peaks between Middlebury Gap and the Winooski River. Now dubbed the Monroe Skyline, this 47.4-mile section is widely considered the soul of the Long Trail, and is a much-sought-after multiday trek. For backpackers who want to sample the best of the Long Trail and have a week or less, this is the trip to take.

The Monroe Skyline links three sections of the Long Trail described elsewhere in this book. For details, see the descriptions for the following three hikes: The Long Trail: Route 125, Middlebury Gap, to the Lincoln-Warren Highway, Lincoln Gap; The Long Trail: Lincoln-Warren Highway, Lincoln Gap, to Route 17, Appalachian Gap; and The Long Trail: Route 17, Appalachian Gap, to the Winooski River.

User Groups
Hikers and dogs. Dogs must be leashed. No wheelchair facilities. This trail should not be attempted in winter except by hikers experienced in mountaineering and prepared for severe winter weather, and is not suitable for bikes, horses, or skis. Hunting is allowed in season, but not near trails.

Access and Fees
Parking and access are free. See specific access information for the Long Trail sections covered separately.

Maps

The waterproof *End-to-End Map of the Long Trail* is available for $8.95 from the Green Mountain Club, as is the *Northern Vermont Hiking Trail Map,* which covers Mount Mansfield, Camel's Hump, Lake Willoughby, Cotton Brook, Little River, the Worcester Range, and Mount Elmore, for $4.95. For topographic area maps, request Bread Loaf, Lincoln, Mount Ellen, Huntington, and Waterbury from USGS Map Sales, Federal Center, Box 25286, Denver, CO 80225, 888/ASK-USGS (888/275-8747), website: http://mapping.usgs.gov.

Directions

You need to shuttle two vehicles for this one-way traverse. To hike south to north, as described here, leave one vehicle in the trailhead parking lot on River Road in North Duxbury (see Directions for Camel's Hump: Long Trail/Bamforth Ridge). Then to reach the trailhead, drive to the large turnout on the south side of Route 125, immediately west of where the Long Trail crosses the road in Middlebury Gap, 5.6 miles east of Ripton and 6.4 miles west of Route 100 in Hancock.

Contact

Green Mountain Club Inc., 4711 Waterbury-Stowe Road, Waterbury Center, VT 05677, 802/244-7037, website: www.greenmountainclub.org.

23 THE LONG TRAIL: LINCOLN-WARREN HIGHWAY, LINCOLN GAP, TO ROUTE 17, APPALACHIAN GAP

between Lincoln Gap and Appalachian Gap

Total distance: 11.6 miles one-way **Hiking time:** 8.5 hours

Difficulty: 9 **Rating:** 10

This 11.6-mile Long Trail stretch traverses the high, narrow ridge of Lincoln Mountain, passing over its several summits, including spectacular 4,006-foot Mount Abraham (see listing in the Southern Green Mountains and Southern Vermont chapter) and two other summits with excellent views. One of the premier sections of the Long Trail, it is also the middle portion of the fabled Monroe Skyline (see previous listing). Although this hike can be done in a long day, many people make a two-day backpacking trip of it or hike it as a link in a longer outing on the Long Trail. The cumulative elevation gain is nearly 2,500 feet.

This is a popular destination in summer and fall, and the shelters tend to fill up quickly on weekends. When above tree line, remember that the fragile alpine vegetation suffers under boots, so stay on the marked trail or rocks. Also be advised that water sources are few along the ridge and generally found only at the shelters (although the spring at the Theron Dean shelter is not reliable in dry seasons).

From the Lincoln-Warren Highway, follow the Long Trail white blazes northbound, gradually beginning the ascent of Mount Abraham. At 1.2 miles, the trail passes a pair of huge boulders named the Carpenters, after two trail workers. At 1.7 miles, the Battell Trail veers left (west), leading two miles to a road; at 0.1 mile farther, the Long Trail reaches the Battell shelter. The trail then climbs more steeply, over rocky terrain and exposed slabs, until it emerges from the trees into the alpine zone atop Abraham, 2.6 miles from the road. The views stretch far down the Green Mountain chain to the south, east to the White Mountains, west to Lake Champlain and the Adirondacks, and north to Lincoln Mountain's other peaks.

At 3.3 miles, a sign indicates the wooded summit of Little

Abe, and 0.1 mile farther the Long Trail crosses Lincoln Peak, at 3,975 feet, where an observation deck to the trail's right offers a panorama. The Long Trail passes through a cleared area above the Sugarbush Valley Ski Area just past the observation deck, bears left, and reenters the forest. The hiking is fairly easy along the ridge, with little elevation shift. At four miles, the Long Trail traverses the wooded summit of Nancy Hanks Peak, passes a Sugarbush chairlift at 4.7 miles, then climbs about 250 feet in elevation to the 4,022-foot Cutts Peak summit, which has good views, at 5.9 miles. Just 0.4 mile farther, the trail passes over the wooded and viewless Mount Ellen summit, at 4,083 feet tied with Camel's Hump for third-highest of Vermont's five official 4,000-footers. (Cutts does not qualify because there is not enough elevation gain and loss between it and Ellen.) The Long Trail almost immediately passes a chairlift for the Sugarbush North Ski Area, bears left along a ski trail for 100 feet, and reenters the woods, descending very rocky ground where footing is difficult.

At 6.7 miles, the Long Trail leaves the national forest, and at 8.1 miles reaches a junction with the Jerusalem Trail, which departs left (west) and continues 2.5 miles to a road. Just 0.1 mile farther, the Long Trail reaches the Barton Trail, which leads to the right (east) 0.2 mile to the Glen Ellen Lodge. The Long Trail then climbs steeply for a short distance to the height of General Stark Mountain (3,662 feet), at 8.5 miles, and reaches the Stark's Nest shelter at 9.1 miles. The Long Trail follows a ski trail briefly, turns left into the woods, crosses a cross-country skiing trail, and then descends steeply to the Theron Dean shelter at 9.8 miles. A path leads a short distance past the shelter to a good view of the mountains to the north. From the shelter, the Long Trail drops steeply, passes another chairlift station at 10 miles, and reaches Route 17 at 11.6 miles.

User Groups

Hikers and dogs. Dogs must be leashed. No wheelchair facilities. This trail should not be attempted in winter except by hikers experienced in mountaineering and prepared for severe winter weather, and is not suitable for bikes, horses, or skis. Hunting is allowed in season, but not near trails.

Access and Fees

Parking and access are free. The Long Trail is closed from Lincoln Gap to Appalachian Gap from mid-April to Memorial Day. The road through Lincoln Gap is not maintained during winter. No-trace camping is permitted within the Green Mountain National Forest, but north of the national forest boundary the Long Trail passes through private land, and camping is prohibited except at the Green Mountain Club's Glen Ellen Lodge cabin, located on the Barton Trail, 0.3 mile east of the Long Trail and 8.2 miles north of Lincoln Gap. From Memorial Day weekend to Columbus Day, a caretaker is on duty and a $6-per-person nightly fee is collected at the Battell shelter on the Long Trail, 1.8 miles north of Lincoln Gap. The Theron Dean shelter is on the Long Trail 9.8 miles north of Lincoln Gap and 1.8 miles south of Appalachian Gap.

Maps

The waterproof *End-to-End Map of the Long Trail* is available for $8.95 from the Green Mountain Club. For topographic area maps, request Lincoln and Mount Ellen from USGS Map Sales, Federal Center, Box 25286, Denver, CO 80225, 888/ASK-USGS (888/275-8747), website: http://mapping.usgs.gov.

Directions

You need to shuttle two vehicles for this one-way traverse. To hike south to north, as described here, leave one vehicle where the Long Trail crosses Route 17 in Appalachian Gap, three miles east of the Huntington Road and six miles west of Route 100 in Irasville. Then drive to where the Long Trail crosses the Lincoln-Warren Highway in Lincoln Gap, 4.7 miles east of Lincoln and 4.1 miles west of Route 100 in Warren. There is parking 0.2 mile west of Lincoln Gap, as well as along the road near the trail crossing.

Contact

Green Mountain National Forest Supervisor, 231 North Main Street, Rutland, VT 05701, 802/747-6700, fax 802/747-6766, website: www.fs.fed.us/r9/gmfl. Green Mountain Club Inc., 4711 Waterbury-Stowe Road, Waterbury Center, VT 05677, 802/244-7037, website: www.greenmountainclub.org.

Chapter 2

© MICHAEL LANZA

Southern Green Mountains and Southern Vermont

Southern Green Mountains and Southern Vermont

The southern Green Mountains do not rise as tall or as rugged as their neighbors to the north. But with relatively easy hiking through gorgeous woods, around scenic ponds, and to the top of occasional summits with long views, the bottom of Vermont is well worth exploring. The Long Trail is much gentler on the knees of hikers and backpackers here, and no less pleasant.

This is also a beautiful part of Vermont to hike in during the peak of fall foliage. And even though the summits aren't as high and most of the hiking here is deep in the woods with no long views, the memory of hiking to places like the Big Branch Wilderness, Baker Peak, Styles Peak, and along the southern Long Trail always triggers a special feeling for me. Plus, some of the higher peaks—Glastenbury Mountain, Stratton Mountain, and Bromley Mountain—have summit towers offering incredible, long views.

This chapter also describes enduringly popular mountains such as Ascutney and secluded, special places such as Silent Cliff, Shrewsbury Peak, Rattlesnake Cliffs, and the Skyline Trail.

The Appalachian Trail coincides with the Long Trail for more than 100 miles, from the Massachusetts line to just north of U.S. 4 in Sherburne Pass. Along the Appalachian Trail, dogs must be kept under control, and bikes, horses, hunting, and firearms are prohibited.

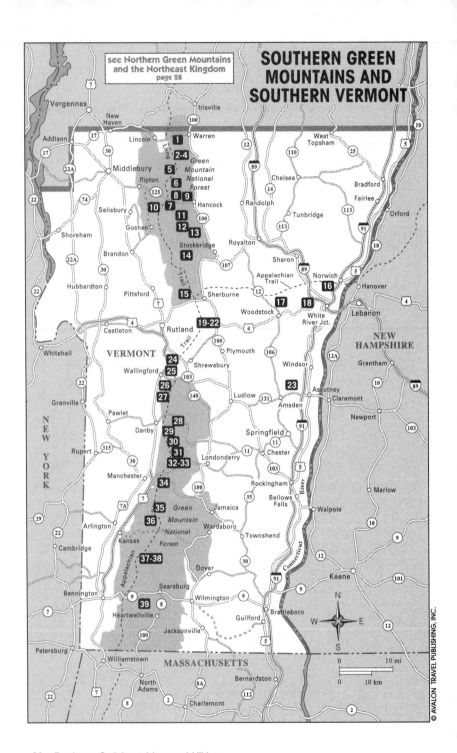

see Northern Green Mountains and the Northeast Kingdom page 28

SOUTHERN GREEN MOUNTAINS AND SOUTHERN VERMONT

© AVALON TRAVEL PUBLISHING, INC.

Contents

◪ MOUNT ABRAHAM

in the Green Mountain National Forest north of Lincoln Gap

Total distance: 5.2 miles round-trip   **Hiking time:** 4 hours

Difficulty: 7   **Rating:** 10

At 4,006 feet in elevation, Mount Abraham is one of just five Vermont summits that rise above 4,000 feet—and one of just four that thrust a rocky crown above the trees. For the other three, check out Killington Peak (see listings in this chapter), Camel's Hump (see listings in previous chapter), and Mount Mansfield (see listings in previous chapter). The 360-degree view from the top of Abraham stretches south along the Green Mountain chain to Killington, west to the Champlain Valley and the Adirondacks, east to the White Mountains on a clear day, and north along this high ridge, anchored by Abraham at its south end. This hike ascends about 1,600 feet.

Remember that the fragile alpine vegetation above tree line suffers under boots, and stay on the marked trail or rocks. From Lincoln Gap, the hike to the summit is a steep, 5.2-mile round-trip. On the ascent, 1.2 miles from the road, the Long Trail passes a pair of huge boulders known as the Carpenters, named for two trail workers. It passes the Battell Trail at 1.7 miles, which veers left (west), leading two miles to a road, and the Battell shelter, 1.8 miles from the road. From Abraham's summit, you can continue north along this level, high ridge to 3,975-foot Lincoln Peak (making this hike's round-trip distance 6.8 miles), where an observation deck just to the trail's right offers views in every direction.

Still feeling strong? Keep hiking north to Cutts Peak, which has good views, and then an easy 0.4 mile beyond Cutts to the wooded and viewless summit of another Vermont 4,000-footer (4,083-foot Mount Ellen), making this marathon hike a 12.6-mile round-trip from Lincoln Gap. Turn around and descend the way you came.

User groups

Hikers and dogs. Dogs must be leashed. No wheelchair facilities. This trail should not be attempted in winter except by hikers experienced in mountaineering and prepared for severe winter weather, and is not suitable for bikes, horses, or skis. Hunting is allowed in season, but not near trails.

Access and Fees
Parking and access are free. The road through Lincoln Gap is not maintained during winter. No-trace camping is permitted within the Green Mountain National Forest. From Memorial Day weekend to Columbus Day, a Green Mountain Club caretaker is on duty and a $6-per-person nightly fee is collected to stay at the Battell shelter, which is on the Long Trail 1.8 miles north of Lincoln Gap. The Long Trail is closed from Lincoln Gap to Appalachian Gap from mid-April to Memorial Day.

Maps
The waterproof *End-to-End Map of the Long Trail* is available for $8.95 from the Green Mountain Club. For topographic area maps, request Lincoln and Mount Ellen from USGS Map Sales, Federal Center, Box 25286, Denver, CO 80225, 888/ASK-USGS (888/275-8747), website: http://mapping.usgs.gov.

Directions
Drive to where the Long Trail crosses the Lincoln-Warren Highway in Lincoln Gap, 4.7 miles east of Lincoln and 4.1 miles west of Route 100 in Warren. There is parking 0.2 mile west of Lincoln Gap, as well as along the road near the trail crossing.

Contact
Green Mountain National Forest Supervisor, 231 North Main Street, Rutland, VT 05701, 802/747-6700, fax 802/747-6766, website: www.fs.fed.us/r9/gmfl. Green Mountain Club Inc., 4711 Waterbury-Stowe Road, Waterbury Center, VT 05677, 802/244-7037, website: www.greenmountainclub.org.

2 EASTWOOD'S RISE AND MOUNT GRANT

in the Green Mountain National Forest south of Lincoln Gap

Total distance: 7.8 miles round-trip   **Hiking time:** 5 hours

Difficulty: 8   **Rating:** 8

This one hike really presents the possibility of two different hikes, one a fairly easy round-trip of just 0.8 mile to Eastwood's Rise, a wide, flat ledge looking west all the way to New York's Adirondacks. Hikers seeking a longer outing can continue on to the Mount Grant summit (3,623 feet), with its view south to the Green Mountains' Bread Loaf Wilderness, for a 7.8-mile round-trip. This entire hike ascends about 1,500 feet.

From Lincoln Gap, follow the white blazes of the Long Trail southbound. The trail passes Eastwood's Rise at 0.4 mile, another overlook called Sunset Ledge at 1.1 miles, and then climbs steadily to Mount Grant at 3.9 miles. Hike back to the parking area along the same route.

User Groups

Hikers and dogs. Dogs must be leashed. No wheelchair facilities. This trail may be difficult to snowshoe because of severe winter weather, and is not suitable for bikes, horses, or skis. Hunting is allowed in season, but not near trails.

Access and Fees

Parking and access are free. The road through Lincoln Gap is not maintained during winter. No-trace camping is permitted within the Green Mountain National Forest. The Cooley Glen shelter is 0.8 mile south of Mount Grant on the Long Trail.

Maps

The waterproof *End-to-End Map of the Long Trail* is available for $8.95 from the Green Mountain Club. For a topographic area map, request Lincoln from USGS Map Sales, Federal Center, Box 25286, Denver, CO 80225, 888/ASK-USGS (888/275-8747), website: http://mapping.usgs.gov.

Directions

Drive to where the Long Trail crosses the Lincoln-Warren Highway in Lincoln Gap, 4.7 miles east of Lincoln and 4.1 miles west of Route 100 in Warren. There is parking 0.2 mile west of Lincoln Gap and along the road near the trail crossing.

Contact

Green Mountain National Forest Supervisor, 231 North Main Street, Rutland, VT 05701, 802/747-6700, fax 802/747-6766, website: www.fs.fed.us/r9/gmfl. Green Mountain Club Inc., 4711 Waterbury-Stowe Road, Waterbury Center, VT 05677, 802/244-7037, website: www.greenmountainclub.org.

❸ MOUNT WILSON

in the Green Mountain National Forest near South Lincoln

Total distance: 8.6 miles round-trip   **Hiking time:** 6 hours

Difficulty: 8   **Rating:** 8

From the ledges just off the Long Trail, near the top of Mount Wilson (3,745 feet), one can take in the long chain of the Green Mountains stretching southward. It's one of the finest views on the Long Trail between Middlebury Gap and Lincoln Gap. From the parking area, much of this hike's approximately 2,000 feet in elevation gain is accomplished on the Emily Proctor Trail, which largely follows an old logging road and crosses a tributary of the New Haven River three times, once on rocks. The crossings could be tricky in high water. The trail ascends moderately for much of its distance, becoming steeper just before reaching the Long Trail at the Emily Proctor shelter, 3.5 miles from the parking area. Turn left and follow the Long Trail northbound for 0.8 mile to the summit of Mount Wilson. An obvious footpath leads a short distance to the overlook.

Returning the way you came, you might consider making the worthwhile side trip to 3,835-foot Bread Loaf Mountain for a sweeping view south and west of the Green Mountains, the Champlain Valley, and the Adirondack Mountains. From the Long Trail junction with the Emily Proctor Trail, hike southbound on the Long Trail for 0.7 mile to the wooded top of Bread Loaf Mountain. Here, the Long Trail swings left, and a side path leads right for 0.1 mile to the overlook. Bagging Bread Loaf Mountain makes this hike's round-trip distance 10 miles. For another hiking option, see the special note with Skylight Pond (see listing in this chapter).

User Groups

Hikers and dogs. Dogs must be leashed. No wheelchair facilities. This trail may be difficult to snowshoe because of severe winter weather, and is not suitable for bikes, horses, or skis. Hunting is allowed in season, but not near trails.

Access and Fees

Parking and access are free. No-trace camping is permitted within the Green Mountain National Forest. The Emily Proctor shelter is located at the Long Trail and Emily Proctor Trail junction, 3.5 miles into this hike. The Skyline Lodge cabin is 0.1 mile east of the Long Trail via the Skylight Pond Trail, and 1.2 mile south of the Bread Loaf Mountain summit.

Maps
The waterproof *End-to-End Map of the Long Trail* is available for $8.95 from the Green Mountain Club. For topographic area maps, request Bread Loaf and Lincoln from USGS Map Sales, Federal Center, Box 25286, Denver, CO 80225, 888/ASK-USGS (888/275-8747), website: http://mapping.usgs.gov.

Directions
From the general store in the center of Lincoln, follow the road to South Lincoln for one mile and turn right at a sign for the Emily Proctor Trail. Drive 1.9 miles (it becomes a dirt road) and continue straight ahead onto South Lincoln Road for another two miles. Turn left onto USFS Road 201 and proceed 0.3 mile to parking on the left.

Contact
Green Mountain National Forest Supervisor, 231 North Main Street, Rutland, VT 05701, 802/747-6700, fax 802/747-6766, website: www.fs.fed.us/r9/gmfl. Green Mountain Club Inc., 4711 Waterbury-Stowe Road, Waterbury Center, VT 05677, 802/244-7037, website: www.greenmountainclub.org.

4 COOLEY GLEN TRAIL/ EMILY PROCTOR TRAIL LOOP

in the Green Mountain National Forest near South Lincoln

Total distance: 12.5 miles round-trip **Hiking time:** 8.5 hours
Difficulty: 9 **Rating:** 8

This 12.5-mile loop traverses three named 3,000-footers, Mounts Cleveland, Roosevelt, and Wilson, the last two of which have good views. The cumulative elevation gain is about 2,500 feet. From the parking area, take the Cooley Glen Trail, which climbs at a moderate grade east, then northeast, paralleling and crossing a stream before reaching the Long Trail at 3.4 miles. The Cooley Glen shelter lies at this trail junction. Turn right (south) on the white-blazed Long Trail, climbing 0.5 mile, steeply at times, to the wooded summit of 3,482-foot Mount Cleveland. The Long Trail follows a ridge through several short dips and climbs for 3.1 miles to the Mount Roosevelt summit, at 3,528 feet, and a spot known as Killington View, with a good outlook south and west of the mountains.

Descending briefly off Roosevelt, the Long Trail reaches the Clark Brook Trail in another 0.4 mile; that trail branches left (east), leading three miles to a road. The Long Trail then ascends 0.8 mile to Mount Wilson (3,745 feet) and the best view on this hike; follow the obvious side path about 100 feet to the left to an open ledge with a long view south down the backbone of the Green Mountains. Just 0.8 mile farther south on the Long Trail, turn right (north) onto the Emily Proctor Trail—near the shelter of the same name—and descend steadily for 3.5 miles to the parking area.

User Groups

Hikers and dogs. Dogs must be leashed. No wheelchair facilities. This trail may be difficult to snowshoe because of severe winter weather, and is not suitable for bikes, horses, or skis. Hunting is allowed in season, but not near trails.

Access and Fees

Parking and access are free. The access road is not maintained for winter access to the trailhead parking lot. No-trace camping is permitted within the Green Mountain National Forest. The Cooley Glen shelter is at the Long Trail and the Cooley Glen Trail junction, 3.4 miles into this hike. The Emily Proctor shelter is located at the Long Trail and Emily Proctor Trail junction, 5.6 miles south of the Cooley Glen shelter.

Maps
The waterproof *End-to-End Map of the Long Trail* is available for $8.95 from the Green Mountain Club. For topographic area maps, request Bread Loaf and Lincoln from USGS Map Sales, Federal Center, Box 25286, Denver, CO 80225, 888/ASK-USGS (888/275-8747), website: http://mapping.usgs.gov.

Directions
From the general store in the center of Lincoln, follow the road to South Lincoln for one mile and turn right at the Emily Proctor Trail sign. Go 1.9 miles (it becomes a dirt road) and continue straight on South Lincoln Road for two miles. Turn left onto USFS Road 201 and drive 0.3 mile to parking on the left.

Contact
Green Mountain National Forest Supervisor, 231 North Main Street, Rutland, VT 05701, 802/747-6700, fax 802/747-6766, website: www.fs.fed.us/r9/gmfl. Green Mountain Club Inc., 4711 Waterbury-Stowe Rd., Waterbury Center, VT 05677, 802/244-7037, website: www.greenmountainclub.org.

⑤ THE LONG TRAIL: ROUTE 125, MIDDLEBURY GAP, TO THE LINCOLN-WARREN HIGHWAY, LINCOLN GAP

in the Green Mountain National Forest between
Middlebury Gap and Lincoln Gap

Total distance: 17.4 miles one-way   **Hiking time:** 2 days

Difficulty: 8   **Rating:** 8

This fairly rugged Long Trail stretch passes over nine named 3,000-foot peaks in 17.4 miles. Although most of this ridge walk is wooded, there are several good, long views of the Green Mountains. This is also the southern section of the famous Monroe Skyline (see listing in the Northern Green Mountains and the Northeast Kingdom chapter). Typical of New England's mountains, the Long Trail here takes you on a roller-coaster ride up and down these peaks in a series of short, often steep steps that can seem endless—while no climb is more than about 500 feet, over the course of this traverse you'll walk some 4,500 feet uphill. But on my own extended Long Trail trek, this section whetted my appetite for the big peaks immediately north—especially the views from spots like Skylight Pond, Bread Loaf Mountain, and Mount Wilson.

a long view from Vermont's Long Trail

From Route 125, the Long Trail northbound climbs steeply for 0.4 mile to a junction with a blue-blazed trail branching right and leading 0.4 mile to Silent Cliff. This easy detour (which adds 0.8 mile to this hike's distance) takes only about 20–30 minutes round-trip and leads to a ledge jutting out over thin air atop Silent Cliff, with a view of Middlebury Gap and the Middlebury Snow Bowl Ski Area, and west to the Champlain Valley and the Adirondacks on a clear day. Immediately before the cliff, a foot-path veers right a few steps to Silent Cave, a passage beneath a massive boulder perched against the mountainside.

From the Silent Cliff Trail junction, the Long Trail swings left and ascends more moderately over 3,040-foot Burnt Hill at 2.1 miles from Route 125, passes the Burnt Hill Trail (which leads west 2.2 miles to a road), and then traverses up and down several summits along the ridge: Kirby Peak (3,140 feet) at 2.7 miles, Mount Boyce (3,323 feet) at 3.6 miles, and Battell Mountain (3,482 feet) at five miles from Route 125. Between Kirby and Boyce, the trail passes Boyce shelter at 3.2 miles. There are a few limited views of surrounding mountains and valleys from along this part of the ridge. At 5.3 miles, the Long Trail is crossed by the Skylight Pond Trail, which leads left (west) 2.3 miles to a road and right (east) 0.1 mile to Skyline Lodge and Skylight Pond, one of the most picturesque spots on this hike. I awoke one morning in Skyline Lodge early enough to catch the predawn sky lit up with vivid red and yellow bands and fog filling the valleys between distant mountain ridges.

From the Skylight Pond Trail, the Long Trail climbs about 400 feet in elevation to Bread Loaf Mountain, where at 6.4 miles a side path leads 0.1 mile to a good overlook south to the long Green Mountains chain and west to the Champlain Valley and Adirondack Mountains. At 7.1 miles, the Long Trail passes the Emily Proctor shelter and the Emily Proctor Trail, which leads north 3.5 miles to a road outside South Lincoln. The Long Trail then ascends about 300 feet to Mount Wilson at 7.9 miles. Do not pass up the obvious path that leads about 100 feet off the trail to ledges where you get a view south down the long backbone of the Greens. The Long Trail descends to a junction with the Clark Brook Trail at 8.7 miles, which leads east three miles to a road; the Long Trail then climbs less than 200 feet to reach the top of 3,528-

foot Mount Roosevelt at 9.1 miles, and a spot called Killington View, with a good prospect south and west toward the mountains.

After several more short climbs and descents, the trail passes over the wooded Mount Cleveland summit (3,482 feet) at 12.2 miles and descends to the Cooley Glen shelter at 12.7 miles. From the shelter, the Long Trail swings west and climbs 500 feet over 0.8 mile to the Mount Grant summit (3,623 feet) at 13.5 miles, where you get a view of the Green Mountains' Bread Loaf Wilderness to the south. The Long Trail continues north along the ridge, passing through an interesting birch forest to a broad view west all the way to the Adirondacks from an open ledge at 17 miles called Eastwood's Rise. The trail drops fairly easily to the Lincoln-Warren Highway in Lincoln Gap.

User Groups
Hikers and dogs. Dogs must be leashed. No wheelchair facilities. This trail may be difficult to snowshoe because of severe winter weather, and is not suitable for bikes, horses, or skis. Hunting is allowed in season, but not near trails.

Access and Fees
Parking and access are free. The road through Lincoln Gap is not maintained during winter. No-trace camping is permitted within the Green Mountain National Forest. North from Route 125 on the Long Trail, it is 5.1 miles to the Skylight Pond Trail, which leads east 0.1 mile to the Skyline Lodge cabin; 6.9 miles to the Emily Proctor shelter; and 12.6 miles to the Cooley Glen shelter (the last is 4.7 miles south of the Lincoln-Warren Highway).

Maps
The waterproof *End-to-End Map of the Long Trail* is available for $8.95 from the Green Mountain Club. For topographic area maps, request Bread Loaf and Lincoln from USGS Map Sales, Federal Center, Box 25286, Denver, CO 80225, 888/ASK-USGS (888/275-8747), website: http://mapping.usgs.gov.

Directions
You need to shuttle two vehicles for this one-way traverse. To hike south to north, as described here, leave one vehicle where the

Long Trail crosses the Lincoln-Warren Highway in Lincoln Gap, 4.7 miles east of Lincoln and 4.1 miles west of Route 100 in Warren. There is parking 0.2 mile west of Lincoln Gap, as well as along the road near the trail crossing. Then drive to the large turnout on Route 125's south side, immediately west of where the Long Trail crosses the road in Middlebury Gap, 5.6 miles east of Ripton and 6.4 miles west of Route 100 in Hancock.

Contact

Green Mountain National Forest Supervisor, 231 North Main Street, Rutland, VT 05701, 802/747-6700, fax 802/747-6766, website: www.fs.fed.us/r9/gmfl. Green Mountain Club Inc., 4711 Waterbury-Stowe Road, Waterbury Center, VT 05677, 802/244-7037, website: www.greenmountainclub.org.

6 SKYLIGHT POND

in the Green Mountain National Forest between
Middlebury Gap and Lincoln Gap

Total distance: 4.8 miles round-trip

Hiking time: 3.2 hours

Difficulty: 5

Rating: 8

I woke up alone in the Skyline Lodge one late October morning, before dawn, and saw fire through a musty window. I stepped outside and stood in the chill for about 45 minutes, watching a spectacular sunrise come to life on the distant eastern horizon, with mountain ridges and fog-filled valleys in the middle distance and the whole scene reflected in Skylight Pond. This is a popular spot, no doubt because the lodge is one of the nicest cabins along the entire trail. This 4.8-mile, round-trip hike can easily be done in a half day, but you just might be tempted to spend the night in the lodge and catch the sunrise. From the parking area, follow the Skylight Pond Trail, which ascends moderately for 2.3 miles to the Long Trail. It crosses the Long Trail and continues 0.1 mile to the lodge, completing a climb of about 1,400 feet. Return the way you came.

Special note: Want to make a longer adventure of it? By shuttling two vehicles, you could combine this hike and Mount Wilson (see listing in this chapter) by taking the Skylight Pond Trail to the pond, the Long Trail north over Bread Loaf Mountain to Mount Wilson, then backtracking on the Long Trail and descending the Emily Proctor Trail, a 9.4-mile trek. From the Skylight Pond Trail parking area, continue driving north on USFS Road 59, bear right onto USFS Road 54, and then turn right onto USFS Road 201 to reach the Emily Proctor Trail parking area.

User Groups

Hikers and dogs. Dogs must be leashed. No wheelchair facilities. This trail may be difficult to snowshoe because of severe winter weather, and is not suitable for bikes, horses, or skis. Hunting is allowed in season, but not near trails.

Access and Fees

Parking and access are free. USFS Road 59 is not maintained in winter. No-trace camping is permitted within the Green Mountain

National Forest. The Skyline Lodge cabin is 0.1 mile off the Long Trail, 2.4 miles into this hike, at the Skylight Pond Trail's end.

Maps

The waterproof *End-to-End Map of the Long Trail* is available for $8.95 from the Green Mountain Club. For topographic area maps, request Bread Loaf and Lincoln from USGS Map Sales, Federal Center, Box 25286, Denver, CO 80225, 888/ASK-USGS (888/275-8747), website: http://mapping.usgs.gov.

Directions

From Route 125, nine miles west of the junction of Routes 125 and 100 in Hancock and 2.8 miles east of Ripton (or 0.8 mile east of the Robert Frost Interpretive Trail parking lot), turn north onto USFS Road 59 and drive about 3.5 miles to parking for the Skylight Pond Trail.

Contact

Green Mountain National Forest Supervisor, 231 North Main Street, Rutland, VT 05701, 802/747-6700, fax 802/747-6766, website: www.fs.fed.us/r9/gmfl. Green Mountain Club Inc., 4711 Waterbury-Stowe Road, Waterbury Center, VT 05677, 802/244-7037, website: www.greenmountainclub.org.

7 ROBERT FROST INTERPRETIVE TRAIL

in the Green Mountain National Forest between Ripton and Hancock

Total distance: 1 mile round-trip **Hiking time:** 0.75 hour

Difficulty: 1 **Rating:** 7

This interpretive trail, beginning from the parking lot, makes a flat, one-mile loop through various microenvironments, including forest, marsh, brooks, and an open meadow with a Green Mountains view. Along the trail are information boards identifying vegetation and containing snippets of verse from the famous New England poet for whom the trail is named. It's a tranquil place to visit under a blanket of snow, although the information boards may be covered by the white stuff, too.

User Groups

Hikers, dogs, skiers, and snowshoers. A portion of this trail is wheelchair accessible. Dogs must be leashed. This trail is not suitable for bikes or horses. Hunting is allowed in season, but not near trails.

Access and Fees

Parking and access are free.

Maps

No map is necessary for this hike. A brochure with information about this and other trails in the national forest's Middlebury and Rochester districts is available from the Green Mountain National Forest Supervisor. For a topographic area map, request Bread Loaf from USGS Map Sales, Federal Center, Box 25286, Denver, CO 80225, 888/ASK-USGS (888/275-8747), website: http://mapping.usgs.gov.

Directions

Drive to the parking area on the south side of Route 125, 9.8 miles west of the junction of Routes 125 and 100 in Hancock and two miles east of Ripton (also 0.1 mile west of the Robert Frost Wayside Area on Route 125).

Contact

Green Mountain National Forest Supervisor, 231 North Main
Street, Rutland, VT 05701, 802/747-6700, fax 802/747-6766, website: www.fs.fed.us/r9/gmfl.

8 SILENT CLIFF
in the Green Mountain National Forest at Middlebury Gap

Total distance: 1.6 miles round-trip   **Hiking time:** 1 hour

Difficulty: 2   **Rating:** 8

The view from atop Silent Cliff, where a ledge juts out into thin air like a defiant chin, takes in a wide sweep of Middlebury Gap, the Middlebury Snow Bowl Ski Area across the gap, and west to the Champlain Valley and the Adirondacks on a clear day. While half the hike is steep, it's just 1.6 miles round-trip and about 400 feet uphill, and is a good trip for young children. From the parking area on Route 125, cross the road and follow the Long Trail northbound, climbing steeply for 0.4 mile. Turn right onto the blue-blazed Silent Cliff Trail, which leads 0.4 mile over much easier terrain to the cliff. Immediately before the cliff is Silent Cave, a steep and tight cavelike passage beneath a massive boulder perched against the mountainside—another attraction guaranteed to fascinate kids. Return the way you came. You might combine this with the Middlebury Gap hike (see listing in this chapter).

User Groups
Hikers and dogs. Dogs must be leashed. No wheelchair facilities. This trail may be difficult to snowshoe because of severe winter weather, and is not suitable for bikes, horses, or skis. Hunting is allowed in season, but not near trails.

Access and Fees
Parking and access are free. No-trace camping is permitted within the Green Mountain National Forest. The Boyce shelter is on the Long Trail, 3.1 miles north of Route 125 and 2.7 miles beyond the junction of the Long and Silent Cliff trails.

Maps
The waterproof *End-to-End Map of the Long Trail* is available for $8.95 from the Green Mountain Club. For a topographic area map, request Bread Loaf from USGS Map Sales, Federal Center, Box 25286, Denver, CO 80225, 888/ASK-USGS (888/275-8747), website: http://mapping.usgs.gov.

Directions
Drive to the large turnout on the south side of Route 125, immediately west of where the Long Trail crosses the road in Middlebury Gap, 5.6 miles east of Ripton and 6.4 miles west of Route 100 in Hancock.

Contact
Green Mountain National Forest Supervisor, 231 North Main Street, Rutland, VT 05701, 802/747-6700, fax 802/747-6766, website: www.fs.fed.us/r9/gmfl. Green Mountain Club Inc., 4711 Waterbury-Stowe Road, Waterbury Center, VT 05677, 802/244-7037, website: www.greenmountainclub.org.

⑨ TEXAS FALLS NATURE TRAIL

in the Green Mountain National Forest between Ripton and Hancock

Total distance: 1 mile round-trip

Hiking time: 1 hour

Difficulty: 2

Rating: 8

Cross USFS Road 39 from the parking turnout, walk down a few steps, and you are at Texas Falls, where Texas Brook charges through a narrow, spectacular gorge. Cross the brook on a wooden bridge—with an excellent view of the gorge—to the start of the one-mile nature trail loop. Bearing left, the trail follows the brook upstream along a well-graded, easy path. Within 0.5 mile, the trail swings right, ascends the hillside briefly, then swings right again, looping back to the start. It's a good hike for introducing young children to the national forest.

User Groups

Hikers, snowshoers, and dogs. Dogs must be leashed. No wheelchair facilities. This trail is not suitable for bikes, horses, or skis. Hunting is allowed in season, but not near trails.

Access and Fees

Parking and access are free. The Texas Falls Recreation Area is closed 10 P.M.–6 A.M. From late fall into spring, USFS Road 39 can be hazardous from snow and ice.

Maps

No map is necessary for this hike. A brochure with information about this and other trails in the national forest's Middlebury and Rochester districts is available from the Green Mountain National Forest Supervisor. For a topographic area map, request Bread Loaf from USGS Map Sales, Federal Center, Box 25286, Denver, CO 80225, 888/ASK-USGS (888/275-8747), website: http://mapping.usgs.gov.

Directions

From Route 125, 3.1 miles west of the junction of Routes 125 and 100 in Hancock and 8.7 miles east of Ripton, turn north onto USFS Road 39 at a sign for Texas Falls. Drive 0.5 mile to a turnout on the left.

Contact

Green Mountain National Forest Supervisor, 231 North Main Street, Rutland, VT 05701, 802/747-6700, fax 802/747-6766, website: www.fs.fed.us/r9/gmfl.

10 FALLS OF LANA AND RATTLESNAKE CLIFFS

in the Green Mountain National Forest and Branbury
State Park south of Middlebury

Total distance: 4.8 miles round-trip

Hiking time: 3 hours

Difficulty: 5

Rating: 9

On a crisp and clear mid-November day, with the leaves long
dead on the ground, I made this 4.8-mile hike past the beautiful
Falls of Lana and up to Rattlesnake Cliffs for a long, late-after-
noon view stretching to New York's Adirondack Mountains. This
moderate hike begins in Branbury State Park and enters the
Green Mountain National Forest, ascending about 1,000 feet to
Rattlesnake Cliffs.

From the parking area, follow the wide woods road 0.5 mile
to the Falls of Lana. Be sure to look for faint side paths leading left to various viewpoints above the falls, which tumble
well over 100 feet through several picturesque cascades and
pools. Many hikers turn back from the Falls of Lana for a
round-trip of just one mile, but this hike continues past the
falls, crossing Sucker Brook in another 0.1 mile. (To the right
of the bridge is the Falls picnic area.) Beyond the bridge, walk
straight ahead onto the North Branch Trail and then bear
right within 100 feet at signs for Rattlesnake Cliffs and the
North Branch Trail. Follow that trail for 0.1 mile, then turn
left at a sign onto the Aunt Jennie Trail. The trail ascends,
steeply in some places, about one mile until you reach the
junction with the Rattlesnake Cliffs Trail. Turn left and follow
that trail 0.1 mile to another junction. Bear left and hike 0.2
mile to the trail's end atop cliffs with a sweeping view that encompasses tiny Silver Lake, the bigger Lake Dunmore, and
the Adirondacks in the distance. Backtrack up the trail about
50 yards to a side path branching to the right; a big tree and
wooden post may be blown down across the path. Continue
on the path downhill for 0.1 mile to another sweeping view,
this one to the south. Backtrack again all the way to the Rattlesnake Cliffs Trail and descend to the parking area the same
way you came.

User Groups

Hikers, snowshoers, and dogs. Dogs must be leashed. No wheelchair facilities. This trail is not suitable for bikes, horses, or skis. Hunting is allowed in season, but not near trails.

Access and Fees

Parking and access are free.

Maps

A basic trail map with state park information is available from the Vermont Department of Forests, Parks, and Recreation. A similar basic trail map with information about these and other trails in the national forest's Middlebury and Rochester districts is available from the Green Mountain National Forest Supervisor. For a topographic area map, request East Middlebury from USGS Map Sales, Federal Center, Box 25286, Denver, CO 80225, 888/ASK-USGS (888/275-8747), website: http://mapping.usgs.gov.

Directions

Drive to the parking area on the east side of Route 53, 5.3 miles north of the junction of Routes 53 and 73 in Forest Dale and 0.4 mile south of the Branbury State Park entrance.

Contact

Branbury State Park, 3570 Lake Dunmore Road, Route 53, Salisbury, VT 05733, 802/247-5925 in summer, 802/483-2001 in winter, or 800/658-1622. Vermont Department of Forests, Parks, and Recreation Commissioner's Office, 103 South Main Street, Waterbury, VT 05671-0601, 802/241-3655, website: www.state.vt .us/anr/fpr. Green Mountain National Forest Supervisor, 231 North Main Street, Rutland, VT 05701, 802/747-6700, fax 802/ 747-6766, website: www.fs.fed.us/r9/gmfl.

11 MIDDLEBURY GAP

in the Green Mountain National Forest at
Middlebury Gap

Total distance: 6.4 miles round-trip   **Hiking time:** 4.5 hours

Difficulty: 7   **Rating:** 7

Hiking the Long Trail south from Middlebury Gap will bring you past a series of views which, while neither sweeping nor grand, make for a pleasant jaunt on a relatively quiet section of the trail. The cumulative elevation gained hiking out and back approaches 2,000 feet. From the road, the trail climbs slightly for 0.4 mile to a side path on the right that leads 0.1 mile to Lake Pleiad and the site of a former shelter, where camping is now prohibited. Continuing south on the white-blazed Long Trail, you cross a pair of ski area trails, and soon reach the first viewpoint, Robert Frost Lookout. The Long Trail goes through some short ups and downs to Monastery Lookout, 2.6 miles from Middlebury Gap. The wooded Worth Mountain summit lies just 0.1 mile farther, and then the trail descends for 0.5 mile past other limited views to South Worth Lookout, 3.2 miles from the highway. Backtracking from here makes a 6.4-mile round-trip. For a slightly longer outing, combine this hike with Silent Cliff (see listing in this chapter).

User Groups

Hikers and dogs. Dogs must be leashed. No wheelchair facilities. This trail may be difficult to snowshoe because of severe winter weather, and is not suitable for bikes, horses, or skis. Hunting is allowed in season, but not near trails.

Access and Fees

Parking and access are free. No-trace camping is permitted within the Green Mountain National Forest. The Sucker Brook shelter is on the Long Trail, 4.4 miles south of Route 125 and 1.2 miles beyond the turnaround point for this hike.

Maps

The waterproof *End-to-End Map of the Long Trail* is available for $8.95 from the Green Mountain Club. For a topographic area map, request Bread Loaf from USGS Map Sales, Federal Center, Box 25286, Denver, CO 80225, 888/ASK-USGS (888/275-8747), website: http://mapping.usgs.gov.

Directions
Drive to the large turnout on the south side of Route 125, immediately west of where the Long Trail crosses the road in Middlebury Gap, 5.6 miles east of Ripton and 6.4 miles west of Route 100 in Hancock.

Contact
Green Mountain National Forest Supervisor, 231 North Main Street, Rutland, VT 05701, 802/747-6700, fax 802/747-6766, website: www.fs.fed.us/r9/gmfl. Green Mountain Club Inc., 4711 Waterbury-Stowe Road, Waterbury Center, VT 05677, 802/244-7037, website: www.greenmountainclub.org.

12 THE LONG TRAIL: ROUTE 73, BRANDON GAP, TO ROUTE 125, MIDDLEBURY GAP

in the Green Mountain National Forest between Brandon Gap and Middlebury Gap

Total distance: 9.8 miles one-way   **Hiking time:** 7.5 hours

Difficulty: 8   **Rating:** 8

The most spectacular natural feature along this 9.8-mile stretch of the Long Trail is the Great Cliff of Mount Horrid, but there are also views from points on the mostly wooded ridge north of Worth Mountain. The trail continues to grow more rugged, with repeated short but fairly steep climbs and descents and significant elevation gains and losses—the biggest being the climb of about 1,200 feet from the road in Brandon Gap to the 3,366-foot Gillespie Peak summit. The cumulative elevation gain on this hike approaches 2,500 feet.

From Route 73, follow the white blazes of the Long Trail northbound. The trail makes quick left and right turns, enters the woods, and begins a steep ascent of 0.6 mile to a junction with a blue-blazed side path leading right 0.1 mile to the view of the gap from the Great Cliff at Mount Horrid. From that junction, the Long Trail ascends more moderately, passing over the wooded Mount Horrid summit (3,216 feet) at 1.2 miles. It then follows the forested ridge, with steep and rocky rises and dips, over Cape Lookoff Mountain at 1.7 miles, Gillespie Peak at 3.2 miles, and Romance Mountain's east summit (3,125 feet) at four miles, before descending to the Sucker Brook shelter at 5.4 miles. The trail then ascends, steeply at times, reaching Worth Mountain at 7.1 miles and follows the ridge north of the mountain past some views to the east and west.

Gradually descending, the Long Trail passes a chairlift station for the Middlebury Snow Bowl, crosses a pair of ski trails, and then reaches a side path on the left at 9.4 miles that leads 0.1 mile to Lake Pleiad and the former site of a shelter; camping is prohibited here. The trail then descends slightly to Route 125 at 9.8 miles.

User Groups

Hikers and dogs. Dogs must be leashed. No wheelchair facilities. This trail may be difficult to snowshoe because of severe winter weather, and is not suitable for bikes, horses, or skis. Hunting is allowed in season, but not near trails.

Access and Fees

Parking and access are free. No-trace camping is permitted within the Green Mountain National Forest. The Sucker Brook shelter is on the Long Trail, 5.4 miles north of Route 73.

Maps

The waterproof *End-to-End Map of the Long Trail* is available for $8.95 from the Green Mountain Club. For topographic area maps, request Mount Carmel and Bread Loaf from USGS Map Sales, Federal Center, Box 25286, Denver, CO 80225, 888/ASK-USGS (888/275-8747), website: http://mapping.usgs.gov.

Directions

You need to shuttle two vehicles for this one-way traverse. To hike south to north, as described here, leave one vehicle in the large turnout on the south side of Route 125, immediately west of where the Long Trail crosses the road in Middlebury Gap, 5.6 miles east of Ripton and 6.4 miles west of Route 100 in Hancock. Then drive to the parking area immediately west of where the Long Trail crosses Route 73 in Brandon Gap, 5.2 miles east of Forest Dale and 9.7 miles west of the Route 100 junction south of Rochester.

Contact

Green Mountain National Forest Supervisor, 231 North Main Street, Rutland, VT 05701, 802/747-6700, fax 802/747-6766, website: www.fs.fed.us/r9/gmfl. Green Mountain Club Inc., 4711 Waterbury-Stowe Road, Waterbury Center, VT 05677, 802/244-7037, website: www.greenmountainclub.org.

🔢 GREAT CLIFF OF MOUNT HORRID

in the Green Mountain National Forest at Brandon Gap

Total distance: 1.2 miles round-trip   **Hiking time:** 1 hour

Difficulty: 2   **Rating:** 8

The Great Cliff of Mount Horrid scowls high above the highway in Brandon Gap, its scarred and crumbling face something of an anomaly in the rounded, generally heavily wooded Green Mountains. This hike, while just 1.2 miles round-trip, climbs quite steeply for about 600 feet to the excellent view of the gap and mountains from the cliff. From Route 73, follow the white blazes of the Long Trail northbound. The trail turns left and right, enters the woods, and climbs for 0.6 mile to a junction with a blue-blazed side path on the right. Follow that side trail 0.1 mile to the view from the cliff. Hike back the same way.

User Groups

Hikers, snowshoers, and dogs. Dogs must be leashed. No wheelchair facilities. This trail is not suitable for bikes, horses, or skis. Hunting is allowed in season, but not near trails.

Access and Fees

Parking and access are free. No-trace camping is permitted within the Green Mountain National Forest. The Sucker Brook shelter is on the Long Trail, 5.4 miles north of Route 73.

Maps

The waterproof *End-to-End Map of the Long Trail* is available for $8.95 from the Green Mountain Club. For a topographic area map, request Mount Carmel from USGS Map Sales, Federal Center, Box 25286, Denver, CO 80225, 888/ASK-USGS (888/275-8747), website: http://mapping.usgs.gov.

Directions

Drive to the parking area immediately west of where the Long Trail crosses Route 73 in Brandon Gap, 5.2 miles east of Forest Dale and 9.7 miles west of the Route 100 junction south of Rochester.

Contact

Green Mountain National Forest Supervisor, 231 North Main Street, Rutland, VT 05701, 802/747-6700, fax 802/747-6766, website: www.fs.fed.us/r9/gmfl. Green Mountain Club Inc., 4711 Waterbury-Stowe Road, Waterbury Center, VT 05677, 802/244-7037, website: www.greenmountainclub.org.

14 THE LONG TRAIL: U.S. 4 TO ROUTE 73, BRANDON GAP

between Sherburne and Brandon Gap

Total distance: 19.9 miles one-way   **Hiking time:** 2 days

Difficulty: 7   **Rating:** 7

This nearly 20-mile Long Trail section is entirely within the woods and fairly flat, with only a few climbs and descents during which elevation gain or loss is no more than 500 or 600 feet—though the cumulative climbing over the entire hike nears 3,000 feet.

The Long Trail was rerouted in September 1999; where it previously crossed U.S. 4 in Sherburne Pass, near the Inn at Long Trail, it now crosses the highway one mile west of the pass. From U.S. 4, pick up the white-blazed Long Trail/Appalachian Trail northbound. It climbs to Willard Gap, rejoining the old route of the Long Trail. To the right, the Appalachian Trail northbound heads toward New Hampshire; for the great view west from the cliff at Deer Leap Trail, walk 0.1 mile down that trail, turn right onto the Deer Leap Trail, and continue less than a mile (this distance is not included in this hike's total distance). This hike turns left and follows the Long Trail northbound along the wooded ridge to Tucker Johnson shelter, 0.4 mile from Willard Gap. The Long Trail continues on fairly easy ground, following an old logging road for awhile. Watch closely for blazes; if you lose the trail, you could find yourself in a maze of woods roads.

The trail crosses the abandoned Chittenden-Pittsfield Road at 3.7 miles, which leads right (east) 0.9 mile to Elbow Road (down which it's another 1.4 miles to Route 100). The Long Trail reaches Rolston Rest shelter 5.4 miles from U.S. 4. The trail climbs over slight rises in the ridge; Chittenden Reservoir may be visible through the trees to the west. At 13.1 miles, the New Boston Trail departs left (west), reaching the David Logan shelter in 0.2 mile, and in 1.2 miles a public road that leads to Chittenden. The trail climbs and dips a bit more beyond this junction—over Mount Carmel without reaching its wooded, 3,361-foot summit, down through Wetmore Gap at 14 miles, over the Bloodroot Mountain east slope, and descending through Bloodroot Gap at

16.5 miles. Passing over one more hill, the Long Trail descends at a very easy grade to Sunrise shelter at 19.8 miles. The trail continues descending another 0.9 mile to Route 73; about 0.2 mile before the highway, you get a good view toward the Great Cliff of Mount Horrid.

User Groups

Hikers and dogs. Dogs must be leashed. No wheelchair facilities. This trail should not be attempted in winter except by hikers prepared for severe winter weather, and is not suitable for bikes, horses, or skis. Hunting is allowed in season, but not near trails.

Access and Fees

Parking and access are free. No-trace camping is permitted within the Green Mountain National Forest; elsewhere, camping is prohibited except at the Green Mountain Club cabins and shelters. The Long Trail is on private land from U.S. 4 to the New Boston Trail, and within the Green Mountain National Forest north of the New Boston Trail. The Tucker Johnson shelter is about 1.4 miles north of U.S. 4; the Rolston Rest shelter is 5.0 miles north of U.S. 4; the David Logan shelter is 0.2 mile south of the Long Trail via the New Boston Trail, which leaves the Long Trail 12.7 miles north of U.S. 4; and the Sunrise shelter is 19 miles north of U.S. 4 (or 0.9 mile south of Route 73).

Maps

The waterproof *End-to-End Map of the Long Trail* is available for $8.95 from the Green Mountain Club. For topographic area maps, request Pico Peak, Chittenden, Mount Carmel, and Rochester from USGS Map Sales, Federal Center, Box 25286, Denver, CO 80225, 888/ASK-USGS (888/275-8747), website: http://mapping.usgs.gov.

Directions

You need to shuttle two vehicles for this one-way traverse. To hike south to north, as described here, leave one vehicle in the parking area immediately west of where the Long Trail crosses Route 73 in Brandon Gap, 5.2 miles east of Forest Dale and 9.7 miles west of the Route 100 junction south of Rochester. Then drive to the Long Trail/Appalachian Trail crossing of U.S. 4, one mile west of Sherburne Pass.

Contact

Green Mountain National Forest Supervisor, 231 North Main Street, Rutland, VT 05701, 802/747-6700, fax 802/747-6766, website: www.fs.fed.us/r9/gmfl. Green Mountain Club Inc., 4711 Waterbury-Stowe Road, Waterbury Center, VT 05677, 802/244-7037, website: www.greenmountainclub.org.

15 DEER LEAP MOUNTAIN
in Sherburne

Total distance: 3.1 miles round-trip   **Hiking time:** 2 hours

Difficulty: 2   **Rating:** 8

Although steep for more than half its course, this 3.1-mile round-trip to Deer Leap Mountain's open ledges meets the criteria for an excellent hike for very young hikers: It feels like a mountain to them, both in relative difficulty and the views which reward them. From the lookout, you peer way down on Sherburne Pass and across to the ski slopes of Pico Peak—and on a clear day, views extend west to New York's Adirondack Mountains. The hike climbs about 600 feet in elevation.

From the parking area, cross U.S. 4 and pick up the blue-blazed Sherburne Pass Trail (formerly the Long Trail northbound), entering the woods just east of the Inn at Long Trail. The trail immediately begins a steep, rocky, 0.5-mile climb to a junction with the Appalachian Trail. Turn onto the Appalachian Trail southbound (actually walking north briefly), and within moments you'll reach the Deer Leap Trail, marked by blue blazes. Follow it up onto a small ridge and through birch forest for 0.9 mile, then turn left onto the Deer Leap Overlook Trail and follow it 0.25 mile to the open ledges overlooking the Coolidge Range and Sherburne Pass.

Backtrack to the Deer Leap Trail. To complete a loop hike, turn north, descending steeply to a brook, then climbing over Big Deer Leap Mountain. The trail will return you to the Appalachian Trail. Turn right, following the Appalachian Trail northbound (though walking southward) back to the Sherburne Pass Trail, then follow the latter back to the trailhead.

User Groups
Hikers and dogs. No wheelchair facilities. This trail may be difficult to snowshoe and is not suitable for skis. Bikes, horses, and hunting are prohibited.

Access and Fees
Parking and access are free.

Maps

For a map of hiking trails, refer to map 5 in the *Map and Guide to the Appalachian Trail in New Hampshire/Vermont,* an eight-map set and guidebook available for $19.95 ($14.95 for the maps alone) from the Appalachian Trail Conference. Or get the water-proof *End-to-End Map of the Long Trail,* available for $8.95 from the Green Mountain Club. For a topographic area map, request Pico Peak from USGS Map Sales, Federal Center, Box 25286, Denver, CO 80225, 888/ASK-USGS (888/275-8747), website: http://mapping.usgs.gov.

Directions

Drive to the parking area across from the Inn at Long Trail, where the Sherburne Pass Trail crosses U.S. 4 at the height of land in Sherburne Pass.

Contact

Green Mountain Club Inc., 4711 Waterbury-Stowe Road, Water-bury Center, VT 05677, 802/244-7037, website: www.greenmountainclub.org. Appalachian Trail Conference, 799 Washington Street, P.O. Box 807, Harpers Ferry, WV 25425-0807, 304/535-6331, website: www.appalachiantrail.org.

16 GILE MOUNTAIN
in Norwich

Total distance: 1.4 miles round-trip   **Hiking time:** 1 hour

Difficulty: 2   **Rating:** 9

With a group of friends, I mountain biked in the Gile Mountain area and hiked to the fire tower on its summit one September afternoon—an uphill climb of not more than 500 feet. From atop the tower, we enjoyed a sweeping panorama south to Mount Ascutney, west to Killington and Abraham, northwest to Camel's Hump, northeast to Mount Moosilauke and Franconia Ridge in the White Mountains, and east across the Connecticut River to the ridge that connects, from north to south, Mount Cube, Smarts Mountain, Holt's Ledge, and Moose Mountain. This is a great place to catch a sunset, especially with the fall foliage at its peak.

Follow the Tower Trail, climbing steadily for 0.4 mile and then crossing power lines. At 0.7 mile, the trail reaches an abandoned fire ranger's cabin. Follow the trail a short distance beyond the cabin to the fire tower. Return the same way you came.

User Groups
Hikers, snowshoers, and dogs. No wheelchair facilities. The last half of this trail is not suitable for bikes or skis, and the entire trail is not suitable for horses. Hunting is allowed in season.

Access and Fees
Parking and access are free.

Maps
For a topographic area map, request Hanover from USGS Map Sales, Federal Center, Box 25286, Denver, CO 80225, 888/ASK-USGS (888/275-8747), website: http://mapping.usgs.gov.

Directions
From I-91, take Exit 13 and follow the signs into Norwich. From Dan and Whit's General Store in the town center, continue straight through town on Main Street for 0.6 mile and turn left

onto Turnpike Road. Drive 0.9 mile and bear left at a fork. In another 1.7 miles, drive straight onto the dirt Lower Turnpike Road. Drive 2.6 miles farther to a turnout on the left for the Gile Mountain Trail.

Contact

Town of Norwich Selectboard, 802/649-0127, email: Selectboard@norwich.vt.us. Town of Norwich Conservation Commission, email: Conservation.Commission@norwich.vt.us.

17 THE SKYLINE TRAIL

in Pomfret

Total distance: 6.3 miles one-way   **Hiking time:** 3.5 hours

Difficulty: 6   **Rating:** 8

The Skyline Trail was conceived in the 1960s by Richard Brett, a local resident who wanted to build a ski trail connecting his homes in Barnard and Woodstock. By gaining the permission of landowners, Brett was able to cut a trail connecting abandoned woods roads, logging roads, and pastures along a woodland ridge between Amity Pond and the Suicide Six Ski Area. Although efforts to complete the route to Woodstock have never succeeded, this trail offers a classic portrait of the Vermont countryside, ranging from dense, quiet woods to farm pastures with long views of green hills. It's a pleasant hike any time of year, but I recommend doing it on cross-country skis after a fresh snowfall, as my wife and I did with two friends a few years ago. There are two long, steep descents, but the tour can be done on standard touring skis by a nordic skier with intermediate skills. Just remember, you could be breaking fresh trail, so don't underestimate how long it can take to ski 6.3 miles. Also remember that the trail is not maintained and you are on private property; access and trail conditions can change at any time. And be careful driving on these Vermont back roads—after we finished skiing here, my wife slid her compact car into a snow bank on her way to retrieve the vehicle we'd left at the trail's start. Fortunately, no one was hurt and passersby helped push the car out of the snow. This trail has fairly short uphill sections, but actually drops about 1,000 in elevation over its course.

From the turnout at the start of the Skyline Trail, follow the trail toward Amity Pond. Where the trail branches left toward the lean-to, take the right fork. The trail soon crosses a broad meadow with long views of the mountains. Beyond the meadow, avoid the local side trails and follow the blue-blazed Skyline Trail. It can be difficult to detect in spots but is generally fairly obvious. It crosses several roads and descends one woods road near its end, before traversing an open hillside, then dropping steeply to Suicide Six.

User Groups

Hikers, snowshoers, skiers, and dogs. No wheelchair facilities or bikes. Horses and hunting are prohibited along much of the trail.

Access and Fees

Parking and access are free. The entire trail lies on private land, so stay on the trail. Access could change, so obey any no trespassing signs. Camping is allowed only in the lean-to shelter at Amity Pond. The trail is generally well marked, but not maintained.

Maps

For a topographic area map, request Woodstock North from USGS Map Sales, Federal Center, Box 25286, Denver, CO 80225, 888/ASK-USGS (888/275-8747), website: http://mapping.usgs.gov.

Directions

You need to shuttle two vehicles for this one-way traverse. To do it north to south, as described here, drive U.S. 4 into Woodstock. Just east of the village center, turn onto Route 12 north, turning right where Route 12 makes a dogleg within 0.2 mile. At 1.3 miles from Route 4, bear right, following signs for the Suicide Six Ski Area, and leave a vehicle in the parking lot. Turn right out of the parking lot, back onto Route 12 south, and drive 0.25 mile to South Pomfret. Turn left onto County Road. Continue another five miles to Hewitt's Corner and take a left at a sign for Sharon. Within 0.25 mile, turn left onto a gravel road. Follow it for roughly two miles; after it bends right and climbs a hill, park in the turnout on the right. The trail begins across the road and is marked by blue trail markers and a sign for the Amity Pond Natural Area.

Contact

The trail is not maintained, but Woodstock Ski Touring Center can provide information, 802/457-6674, website: www.woodstock-inn.com.

18 QUECHEE GORGE

in Quechee Gorge State Park

Total distance: 2.2 miles round-trip   **Hiking time:** 1.2 hours

Difficulty: 2   **Rating:** 8

This 150-foot-deep, narrow gorge along the Ottauquechee River
has long attracted tourists to a bridge on U.S. 4 spanning the
gorge. I first ventured into the gorge on cross-country skis several
years ago, making this easy, 2.2-mile loop along the gorge and
through the woods of tiny Quechee Gorge State Park. If you're
skiing and interested in a longer outing, start from Wilderness
Trails, which maintains a ski trail system adjacent to this loop.
From the parking area, walk down the steps in front of the gift
shop to the gorge trail and turn left (south), passing under the
highway bridge. Follow the well-graded trail above the gorge downhill about a half mile to a bend in the river, where there is a bench.
Turn left, continue about 0.2 mile along the river, walk up a small
hill with good views of the river, and cross a small footbridge.
Turn left onto the Beaver Dam Trail, marked by red wooden
blocks on trees, which winds up through the state park, leaving the
park boundaries briefly and crossing private property. The trail
leads a mile to U.S. 4, at the state park campground entrance and
0.5 mile east of the bridge. You can walk along the road back to
the start of this hike or, especially if on skis, cross the highway and
walk behind the Wildflowers Restaurant to an easy ski trail. Turn
left and follow it 0.5 mile back to the gorge trail. Turn left and
continue a short distance back to the start of this hike.

User Groups

Hikers, dogs, skiers, and snowshoers. No wheelchair facilities.
This trail is not suitable for bikes or horses. Hunting is prohibited.

Access and Fees

Parking and access are free, except that skiers must pay $5 per
person at Wilderness Trails to cover costs of grooming the trails.
Most of this hike is within Quechee Gorge State Park, but the
Beaver Dam Trail briefly exits the state park onto private property; take care not to wander off the trail.

Maps

Get a map of ski trails at Wilderness Trails, behind the Marshland Farm. To reach Wilderness Trails, take Dewey's Mill Road, between the gift shops on the east side of the bridge, and follow it a mile; snowshoes and cross-country skis for adults and children can be rented there. For a topographic area map, request Quechee from USGS Map Sales, Federal Center, Box 25286, Denver, CO 80225, 888/ASK-USGS (888/275-8747), website: http://mapping.usgs.gov.

Directions

From I-89 southbound, take Exit 1 onto U.S. 4 west and drive 2.5 miles to the east side of the U.S. 4 bridge over Quechee Gorge. From I-89 northbound, take Exit 1 and drive 3.2 miles to the gorge. Park at the gift shop or information booth on the bridge's east side.

Contact

Quechee Gorge State Park, 190 Dewey Mills Road, White River Junction, VT 05001, 802/295-2990 in summer, 802/885-8891 in winter, or 800/299-3071. Vermont Department of Forests, Parks, and Recreation Commissioner's Office, 103 South Main Street, Waterbury, VT 05671-0601, 802/241-3655, website: www.state.vt .us/anr/fpr. Friends of the Quechee Gorge, P.O. Box Q, Quechee, VT 05059.

19 KILLINGTON PEAK: BUCKLIN TRAIL
in Mendon and Sherburne

Total distance: 7.4 miles round-trip   **Hiking time:** 6 hours

Difficulty: 9   **Rating:** 10

This 7.4-mile hike provides a route of moderate distance and difficulty up Vermont's second-highest peak, 4,241-foot Killington, where the barren, rocky summit boasts one of the finest panoramas in the state. From the summit, where there are radio transmission facilities and a fire tower, the views extend to Mount Mansfield to the north, numerous other Green Mountains peaks to the north and south, Lake Champlain and the Adirondack Mountains to the west, Mount Ascutney to the southeast, and the White Mountains to the northeast. The vertical ascent is about 2,400 feet.

From the parking area, take the blue-blazed Bucklin Trail. It follows an abandoned logging road, first on the north bank of Brewers Brook, then the south bank, for nearly two miles. It grows steeper beyond the logging road, reaching the white-blazed Long Trail/Appalachian Trail at 3.3 miles. Continue uphill on the Long Trail southbound, reaching the Cooper Lodge in 0.2 mile; just beyond it, the Long Trail swings right, and the spur trail to Killington's summit continues straight ahead. Hike up the very steep and rocky spur trail for 0.2 mile to the summit. Hike back along the same route.

User Groups
Hikers and dogs. No wheelchair facilities. This trail should not be attempted in winter except by hikers experienced in mountaineering and prepared for severe winter weather, and is not suitable for skis. Bikes, horses, and hunting are prohibited.

Access and Fees
Parking and access are free. Most of this hike takes place on private land. Camping is prohibited except at the Green Mountain Club cabins and shelters. The Cooper Lodge cabin is located on the Long Trail, 0.1 mile south of the Bucklin Trail junction.

Maps

For a map of hiking trails, refer to map 6 in the *Map and Guide to the Appalachian Trail in New Hampshire/Vermont,* an eight-map set and guidebook available for $19.95 ($14.95 for the maps alone) from the Appalachian Trail Conference. Or get the waterproof *End-to-End Map of the Long Trail,* available for $8.95 from the Green Mountain Club. For a topographic area map, request Killington Peak from USGS Map Sales, Federal Center, Box 25286, Denver, CO 80225, 888/ASK-USGS (888/275-8747), website: http://mapping.usgs.gov.

Directions

From U.S. 4, 5.1 miles east of the northern junction of U.S. 4 and U.S. 7 in Rutland and 4.1 miles west of the Inn at Long Trail in Sherburne Pass, turn south onto Wheelerville Road. Follow it for 4.1 miles to a turnout on the left.

Contact

Green Mountain Club Inc., 4711 Waterbury-Stowe Road, Waterbury Center, VT 05677, 802/244-7037, website: www.greenmountainclub.org. Appalachian Trail Conference, 799 Washington Street, P.O. Box 807, Harpers Ferry, WV 25425-0807, 304/535-6331, website: www.appalachiantrail.org.

20 KILLINGTON PEAK: SHERBURNE PASS TRAIL
in Sherburne

Total distance: 11.2 miles round-trip   **Hiking time:** 8 hours

Difficulty: 8   **Rating:** 10

Although a fairly challenging hike of more than 11 miles, the Sherburne Pass Trail from Sherburne Pass presents a good route to the crown of Vermont's second-highest peak, 4,241-foot Killington. With the trailhead at 2,150 feet, the vertical ascent is about 2,100 feet, less than taking the Bucklin Trail up Killington (see previous listing). And this hike also offers the option of bagging Pico Peak. On the craggy Killington summit, where there are radio transmission facilities and a fire tower, the 360-degree views encompass Mount Mansfield to the north, numerous other Green Mountains peaks to the north and south, Lake Champlain and the Adirondack Mountains to the west, Mount Ascutney to the southeast, and the White Mountains to the northeast.

From the parking area at Sherburne Pass, follow a short spur trail to the blue-blazed Sherburne Pass Trail southbound (this was a stretch of the Long Trail/Appalachian Trail until the national scenic trail was rerouted in September 1999 to the west side of Pico Mountain). Alternatively, you could walk east along U.S. 4 a short distance and turn right onto the Sherburne Pass Trail southbound. It climbs gradually for 0.6 mile to a side path that leads 0.1 mile right to a view from the top of a chairlift and an alpine slide at the Pico Ski Area. Continuing its steady ascent, the Sherburne Pass Trail reaches a ski trail at two miles and follows it for 300 yards before reentering the woods. At 2.5 miles from the pass, the Sherburne Pass Trail reaches Pico Camp. A side path, Pico Link, leads 0.4 mile up steep and rocky ground from behind Pico Camp to the 3,957-foot Pico Mountain summit, where there are good views (adding 0.8 mile to this hike's distance). Continue on the Sherburne Pass Trail southbound, mostly contouring along the rugged ridge to Killington Peak. About a half mile south of Pico Camp, you reach a junction with the white-blazed Long Trail/Appalachian Trail. Walk southbound on it. At about 5.5 miles from Sherburne Pass, the trail reaches

Cooper Lodge and the junction with the spur trail to Killington's summit. Turn left and climb the very steep and rocky spur for 0.2 mile to the open summit. Return the way you came.

User Groups

Hikers and dogs. No wheelchair facilities. This trail should not be attempted in winter except by hikers experienced in mountaineering and prepared for severe winter weather, and is not suitable for skis. Bikes, horses, and hunting are prohibited.

Access and Fees

Parking and access are free. Parts of this hike are on private land. Camping is prohibited except at the Green Mountain Club cabins and shelters. The Pico Camp cabin is at the junction of the Sherburne Pass Trail and Pico Link, 2.5 miles south of Sherburne Pass and 0.5 mile north of the junction of the Long Trail/Appalachian Trail and the Sherburne Pass Trail. The Cooper Lodge cabin is located on the Long Trail, 0.1 mile south of the Bucklin Trail junction and 2.5 miles south of the junction of the Sherburne Pass and Long Trails; from Cooper Lodge, it is 5.5 miles to Sherburne Pass and U.S. 4 via the Sherburne Pass Trail and 6.3 miles to U.S. 4 via the Long Trail.

Maps

For a map of hiking trails, refer to map 6 in the *Map and Guide to the Appalachian Trail in New Hampshire/Vermont,* an eight-map set and guidebook available for $19.95 ($14.95 for the maps alone) from the Appalachian Trail Conference. Or get the waterproof *End-to-End Map of the Long Trail,* available for $8.95 from the Green Mountain Club. For topographic area maps, request Killington Peak and Pico Peak from USGS Map Sales, Federal Center, Box 25286, Denver, CO 80225, 888/ASK-USGS (888/275-8747), website: http://mapping.usgs.gov.

Directions

Drive to the parking area across from the Inn at Long Trail, where the Sherburne Pass Trail (formerly the Long Trail/Appalachian Trail) crosses U.S. 4 at the height of land in Sherburne Pass.

Contact

Green Mountain Club Inc., 4711 Waterbury-Stowe Road, Waterbury Center, VT 05677, 802/244-7037, website: www.greenmountainclub.org. Appalachian Trail Conference, 799 Washington Street, P.O. Box 807, Harpers Ferry, WV 25425-0807, 304/535-6331, website: www.appalachiantrail.org.

21 THE LONG TRAIL: ROUTE 103 TO U.S. 4
between Shrewsbury and Sherburne

Total distance: 17.4 miles one-way

Hiking time: 2 days

Difficulty: 9

Rating: 9

For someone hiking the entire Long Trail from south to north, this stretch is where the trail begins to metamorphose from a casual walk in the woods with occasional views to a more committing and rugged tromp through the mountains. The difference in elevation from Route 103 to the summit of Killington Peak—Vermont's second-tallest mountain at 4,241 feet—is about 3,400 feet. The views in every direction from the rocky, open Killington summit, where there are radio transmission facilities and a fire tower, encompass Mount Mansfield to the north, numerous other Green Mountains peaks to the north and south, Lake Champlain and the Adirondack Mountains to the west, Mount Ascutney to the southeast, and the White Mountains to the northeast. Remember that weather at the higher elevations can turn wintry in any month.

From the parking area on Route 103, the white-blazed Long Trail, which coincides here with the Appalachian Trail, crosses the highway and employs wooden stepladders to get over barbed wire fencing enclosing a field. Crossing the field into the woods, the trail follows a woods road and climbs steeply through a narrow, boulder-strewn ravine. Above the ravine, the Long Trail passes a view to the south and west (0.4 mile from Route 103) and then descends to another woods road a mile from Route 103. To the right, a short distance down the road, is the Clarendon shelter. The Long Trail crosses the road and a brook and ascends Beacon Hill at 1.5 miles, where there is a view south from an open area at the summit. The trail descends again, crossing Lottery Road at 1.9 miles and the dirt Keiffer Road at 3.6 miles. After following Northam Brook, it turns right onto Cold River Road (also called Lower Road), at 3.9 miles. The Long Trail soon reenters the woods, following a ridge high above the Cold River, and descends steeply to cross the river's east branch on rocks, which could be tricky in times of high water. After paralleling the river's west branch, the trail crosses Upper Cold River Road at 5.4 miles.

At six miles, turn left onto a dirt road, walk over a bridge, and then turn immediately right into the woods. The trail crosses one more road before reaching the Governor Clement shelter at 6.9 miles from Route 103. Passing the shelter, the trail follows a flat woods road for less than a half mile and then starts the long climb up Little Killington and Killington Peak, becoming increasingly rockier, with difficult footing, as the trail narrows through a dense spruce forest. You gain nearly 2,400 feet in elevation. At nine miles, the Long Trail crosses two small brooks that I've seen flowing well even during a dry autumn. The Long Trail crosses a ski area trail on Killington and then reaches a junction at 9.8 miles with the Shrewsbury Peak Trail (see listing in this chapter), which bears right and leads two miles to Shrewsbury Peak, while the Long Trail swings left.

After crossing another ski trail, the hiking grows easier, contouring around the south and west slopes of Killington Peak. At 10.9 miles, a side path bears right and climbs very steeply, over rocky terrain, 0.2 mile to the Killington summit (included in this hike's mileage). Leave your pack behind for this side trip. The Long Trail passes the Cooper Lodge and descends for 0.2 mile before swinging north again. At 13.3 miles, the blue-blazed Sherburne Pass Trail diverges right, following the former route of the Long Trail for 0.5 mile to Pico Camp (there, a blue-blazed side trail, the Pico Link, leads steeply uphill for 0.4 mile to the Pico summit, where there are views and a chairlift station), and, beyond the Pico Camp, continues three more miles to U.S. 4 at Sherburne Pass.

This hike instead follows the new route of the Long Trail/Appalachian Trail—opened in September 1999—a relocation done to avoid ski resort development on Pico Peak. Descending through a birch glade, the trail crosses a stream and a bridge across a brook. At 4.4 miles beyond Cooper Lodge, a spur trail leads 0.1 mile to the Churchill Scott shelter, which sleeps 10 and has a tent platform nearby. It's another 2.4 miles on the Long Trail/Appalachian Trail from Churchill Scott shelter to where the trail crosses Route 4 about a mile west of Sherburne Pass.

User Groups

Hikers and dogs. No wheelchair facilities. This trail should not be attempted in winter except by hikers prepared for severe winter weather, and is not suitable for skis. Bikes, horses, and hunting are prohibited.

Access and Fees
Parking and access are free. Except for a patch of state-owned land on Killington Peak, this hike is on private land; camping is prohibited except at the Green Mountain Club shelters. From Route 103, it is one mile north to the Clarendon shelter, reached via a short walk down a woods road from the Long Trail; 6.8 miles to the Governor Clement shelter; 11.1 miles to the Cooper Lodge cabin; and 15.5 miles to Churchill Scott shelter. The Pico Camp cabin is on the Sherburne Pass Trail, 0.5 mile north of its junction with the Long Trail and 3.0 miles south of U.S. 4.

Maps
For a map of hiking trails, refer to map 6 in the *Map and Guide to the Appalachian Trail in New Hampshire/Vermont,* an eight-map set and guidebook available for $19.95 ($14.95 for the maps alone) from the Appalachian Trail Conference. Or get the waterproof *End-to-End Map of the Long Trail,* available for $8.95 from the Green Mountain Club. For topographic area maps, request Rutland, Killington Peak, and Pico Peak from USGS Map Sales, Federal Center, Box 25286, Denver, CO 80225, 888/ASK-USGS (888/275-8747), website: http://mapping.usgs.gov.

Directions
You need to shuttle two vehicles for this one-way traverse. To hike south to north, as described here, leave one vehicle where the Long Trail/Appalachian Trail crosses U.S. 4, one mile west of Sherburne Pass. Then drive to the parking area where the trail crosses Route 103, two miles east of U.S. 7 in Clarendon, and three miles west of Cuttingsville.

Contact
Green Mountain Club Inc., 4711 Waterbury-Stowe Road, Waterbury Center, VT 05677, 802/244-7037, website: www.greenmountainclub.org. Appalachian Trail Conference, 799 Washington Street, P.O. Box 807, Harpers Ferry, WV 25425-0807, 304/535-6331, website: www.appalachiantrail.org.

22 SHREWSBURY PEAK

in Coolidge State Forest outside North Shrewsbury

Total distance: 3.6 miles round-trip   **Hiking time:** 2.5 hours

Difficulty: 4   **Rating:** 8

On a mid-November day, with an inch of snow turning everything white, I hiked to the Shrewsbury Peak summit and enjoyed wonderfully long views in a wide sweep to the northeast, east, and south. In the clear air I saw all the way to Franconia Ridge in the White Mountains, Mount Ascutney to the east, Mount Monadnock to the southeast, and a long chain of the Green Mountains to the south. Through openings in the trees looking north, I even caught a glimpse of Killington (which can be reached via the Shrewsbury Peak Trail for a scenic if quite rugged round-trip hike of 10.2 miles). This hike climbs about 1,400 feet.

The Shrewsbury Peak Trail is unmarked but obvious and begins from the stone wall at the rear of the parking lot. Within 0.2 mile, it passes in front of a lean-to. Follow the blue blazes over moderate terrain, which grows steeper as the trail ascends into the subalpine hemlock and spruce forest. At 1.8 miles, you emerge at an open area at the summit. To complete this hike, return the way you came. To continue to Killington Peak, follow the Shrewsbury Peak Trail northward. In two miles, turn right (north) on the white-blazed Long Trail and follow it 1.1 miles to the Killington Peak Spur Trail. Turn right and climb very steeply 0.2 mile to the Killington summit.

User Groups

Hikers, snowshoers, and dogs. Dogs must be leashed. No wheelchair facilities. This trail is not suitable for bikes, horses, or skis. Hunting is allowed in season.

Access and Fees

Parking and access are free. The CCC Road can be difficult to drive, especially from the east, in muddy or icy conditions.

Maps

The waterproof *End-to-End Map of the Long Trail* is available for

$8.95 from the Green Mountain Club. For a topographic area map, request Killington Peak from USGS Map Sales, Federal Center, Box 25286, Denver, CO 80225, 888/ASK-USGS (888/275-8747), website: http://mapping.usgs.gov.

Directions

From Route 100, 3.1 miles south of its junction with U.S. 4 in West Bridgewater, and 2.2 miles north of its junction with Route 100A in Plymouth Union, turn west onto the dirt CCC Road at a sign for Meadowsweet Herb Farm. Drive 3.4 miles to a parking area on the right at a sign for the Coolidge State Forest. Or from the center of North Shrewsbury, pick up the CCC Road (marked by a sign) heading east, which begins as pavement and turns to dirt. At 1.1 miles, bear right at a fork and continue 1.6 miles farther to the parking area on the left.

Contact

Vermont Department of Forests, Parks, and Recreation Commissioner's Office, 103 South Main Street, Waterbury, VT 05671-0601, 802/241-3655, website: www.state.vt.us/anr/fpr. Green Mountain Club Inc., 4711 Waterbury-Stowe Road, Waterbury Center, VT 05677, 802/244-7037, website: www.greenmountainclub.org.

23 MOUNT ASCUTNEY
in Ascutney State Park in Windsor

Total distance: 6.8 miles round-trip   **Hiking time:** 4.5 hours

Difficulty: 8   **Rating:** 9

Mount Ascutney, at 3,150 feet, belongs to a class of small New England mountains that rise much higher than any piece of earth surrounding them—peaks like Monadnock and Cardigan in New Hampshire and Wachusett in Massachusetts. The eroded core of a volcano that once rose to 20,000 feet, Ascutney soars above the Connecticut River Valley. Its observation tower offers excellent views of the Green Mountains to the west, Monadnock to the southeast, Mounts Sunapee and Cardigan to the northeast, and the White Mountains beyond. The first trail up Ascutney was cut in 1825; today, several paths run up the mountain. This loop hike climbs about 2,400 feet in elevation.

Follow the Brownsville Trail's white blazes, climbing steadily along a wide woods path. At 1.1 miles, the trail passes by the Norcross Quarry remains on the right, where granite was mined until 1910. The trail continues upward, passing a short side path at 1.3 miles leading to an overlook. A second lookout is reached at two miles, offering a view eastward. At 2.3 miles, the trail crosses a grassy area atop wooded North Peak (2,660 feet). After reaching the Windsor Trail junction (on the left) at 2.9 miles, bear right for the summit. Just 0.1 mile beyond that junction, you reach the remains of the Stone Hut, a former shelter. An unmarked trail leads left 0.7 mile to the Ascutney auto road, and to the right, a short path leads to Brownsville Rock, which offers good views north.

Continue up the Windsor Trail 0.2 mile to the summit observation tower. Descend the same route for 0.3 mile and then turn right to follow the white-blazed Windsor Trail down. The trail crosses the two branches of Mountain Brook and then parallels the brook on a wide, old woods road through a wild drainage. At 2.6 miles below the summit, you reach Route 44A and the parking area for the Windsor Trail. If you have no vehicle here, turn left and follow 44A onto Route 44 west for 0.9 mile to the start of this hike.

User Groups

Hikers and snowshoers. No wheelchair facilities. This trail is not suitable for bikes, horses, or skis. Dogs are not allowed in day-use areas such as picnic areas, but are unrestricted on trails. Hunting is allowed in season.

Access and Fees

Parking and access are free. Trails are closed during the spring mud season, usually mid-April to mid-May.

Maps

The Ascutney Trails Association publishes an Ascutney guide-book and map that costs $5. A free, basic map is available at park entrances for virtually all state parks. For a topographic area map, request Mount Ascutney from USGS Map Sales, Federal Center, Box 25286, Denver, CO 80225, 888/ASK-USGS (888/275-8747), website: http://mapping.usgs.gov.

Directions

If you have two vehicles, drive one to the Windsor Trail parking area at the end of this hike, reducing this hike's distance by the one mile of paved road separating the trailheads; otherwise, just note the location of the Windsor Trail on your way to the start of the Brownsville Trail. From the north, take I-91 to Exit 9 and then U.S. 5 south into the center of Windsor; from the south, take I-91 to Exit 8 and then U.S. 5 north into Windsor. At the junction of U.S. 5 and Route 44 in Windsor, turn west onto Route 44 and follow it for 3.3 miles to its junction with Route 44A. The Windsor Trail parking area is just 100 yards down Route 44A, on the right. Continue west on Route 44 for 0.9 mile to parking on the left side of the road for the Brownsville Trail.

Contact

Ascutney State Park, Box 186, HCR 71, 1826 Black Mountain Road, Windsor, VT 05089, 802/674-2060 in summer, 802/885-8891 in winter, or 800/299-3071. Vermont Department of Forests, Parks, and Recreation Commissioner's Office, 103 South Main Street, Waterbury, VT 05671-0601, 802/241-3655, website: www.state.vt.us/anr/fpr. Ascutney Trails Association, George Smith, Jr., P.O. Box 119, Hartland, VT 05048.

24 CLARENDON GORGE AND AIRPORT LOOKOUT
between Shrewsbury and Clarendon

Total distance: 1.8 miles round-trip

Hiking time: 1.2 hours

Difficulty: 2

Rating: 7

For the view down into Clarendon Gorge, one of the two attractions on this hike, you need only walk southbound on the white-blazed Long Trail/Appalachian Trail for 0.1 mile to the suspension bridge spanning the dramatic chasm. But the added uphill climb of less than a mile and several hundred feet to Airport Lookout is worth the effort. Its open ledges atop low cliffs afford a view west to the Rutland Airport, the valley that U.S. 7 runs through, and the southern Adirondacks. Be careful scrambling around on these ledges; I nearly took a nasty fall there myself. From Airport Lookout, backtrack the way you came.

User Groups
Hikers, snowshoers, and dogs. No wheelchair facilities. This trail is not suitable for skis. Bikes, horses, and hunting are prohibited.

Access and Fees
Parking and access are free.

Maps
For a map of hiking trails, refer to map 6 in the *Map and Guide to the Appalachian Trail in New Hampshire/Vermont,* an eight-map set and guidebook available for $19.95 ($14.95 for the maps alone) from the Appalachian Trail Conference. Or get the waterproof *End-to-End Map of the Long Trail,* available for $8.95 from the Green Mountain Club. For a topographic area map, request Rutland from USGS Map Sales, Federal Center, Box 25286, Denver, CO 80225, 888/ASK-USGS (888/275-8747), website: http://mapping.usgs.gov.

Directions
Drive to the parking area on Route 103, three miles west of Cuttingsville and two miles east of U.S. 7 in Clarendon.

Contact

Green Mountain Club Inc., 4711 Waterbury-Stowe Road, Waterbury Center, VT 05677, 802/244-7037, website: www.greenmountainclub.org. Appalachian Trail Conference, 799 Washington Street, P.O. Box 807, Harpers Ferry, WV 25425-0807, 304/535-6331, website: www.appalachiantrail.org.

25 THE LONG TRAIL: ROUTE 140, WALLINGFORD GULF, TO ROUTE 103, CLARENDON GORGE

between Shrewsbury and Clarendon

Total distance: 6.3 miles one-way   **Hiking time:** 3.5 hours

Difficulty: 6   **Rating:** 7

In September 1999, the Long Trail was rerouted in this area and now ascends the south ridge of 2,262-foot Bear Mountain on this stretch, an improvement over the previous route because it now leads to a great view of the Otter Creek Valley. But this approximately 6.3-mile stretch of the Long and Appalachian Trails is still largely a pleasant walk in the woods and perhaps a safe and moderate route for a beginning winter hiker or snowshoer. The cumulative elevation gain is about 1,200 feet.

From Route 140, follow the Long Trail northbound up Bear Mountain; don't miss the short spur trail to an open ledge overlooking the Otter Creek Valley to the south. The Long Trail continues north, contouring just below the ridgeline, descends the steep north side of Bear Mountain, crosses a beaver meadow, and then follows a woods road to rejoin the old route of the Long Trail just south of Minerva Hinchey shelter. At about 2.6 miles into this hike, a side path leads to the shelter. Beyond it, the Long Trail climbs over a low, wooded hill and descends and passes through Spring Lake Clearing, 3.2 miles from Route 140. It follows a wooded ridge to Airport Lookout at 4.5 miles, where open ledges atop low cliffs offer a view west of the Rutland Airport, the valley that U.S. 7 runs through, and the southern Adirondacks. Descending, the trail reaches Clarendon Gorge, crossing the gorge on a suspension bridge that offers a dramatic view down into the chasm. Just 0.1 mile farther, you reach Route 103.

User Groups

Hikers, snowshoers, and dogs. No wheelchair facilities. This trail is not suitable for skis. Bikes, horses, and hunting are prohibited.

Access and Fees

Parking and access are free. Except for a patch of state-owned land at Clarendon Gorge, this hike is on private land; camping is prohibited except at the Green Mountain Club Minerva Hinchey shelter, reached via a short side path off the Long Trail, 2.6 miles north of Route 140.

Maps

For a map of hiking trails, refer to map 6 in the *Map and Guide to the Appalachian Trail in New Hampshire/Vermont,* an eight-map set and guidebook available for $19.95 ($14.95 for the maps alone) from the Appalachian Trail Conference. Or get the water-proof *End-to-End Map of the Long Trail,* available for $8.95 from the Green Mountain Club. For topographic area maps, request Wallingford and Rutland from USGS Map Sales, Federal Center, Box 25286, Denver, CO 80225, 888/ASK-USGS (888/275-8747), website: http://mapping.usgs.gov.

Directions

You need to shuttle two vehicles for this one-way traverse. To hike south to north, as described here, leave one vehicle in the parking area on Route 103, two miles east of U.S. 7 in Clarendon, and three miles west of Cuttingsville. Then drive to where the Long Trail/Appalachian Trail crosses Route 140, about 2.8 miles east of U.S. 7 in Wallingford and about 3.7 miles west of the junction of Routes 140, 155, and 103 in East Wallingford.

Contact

Green Mountain Club Inc., 4711 Waterbury-Stowe Road, Waterbury Center, VT 05677, 802/244-7037, website: www.greenmountainclub.org. Appalachian Trail Conference, 799 Washington Street, P.O. Box 807, Harpers Ferry, WV 25425-0807, 304/535-6331, website: www.appalachiantrail.org.

26 WHITE ROCKS CLIFF

in the Green Mountain National Forest east of Wallingford

Total distance: 2.6 miles round-trip   **Hiking time:** 2 hours

Difficulty: 7   **Rating:** 8

From the White Rocks Recreation Area, follow the Keewaydin Trail steeply uphill. It soon passes a newly rerouted stretch of the northbound Long Trail bearing left; continue up the Keewaydin, and at 0.8 mile from the trailhead you'll reach a junction with the Greenwall Spur, a trail leading left 0.5 mile to the Greenwall shelter. Turn right (south) on the Long Trail, hike 0.3 mile, and then turn right (west) on the White Rocks Cliff Trail. This trail descends steeply for 0.2 mile and ends at the top of the cliffs, with good views of the valley south of Wallingford. There are numerous footpaths around the cliffs, but take care because the rock is loose and footing can be dangerous. Return the way you came. The cumulative elevation gain on this hike is approximately 1,500 feet.

User Groups

Hikers and dogs. Dogs must be leashed. No wheelchair facilities. This trail may be difficult to snowshoe and is not suitable for skis. Bikes, horses, and hunting are prohibited.

Access and Fees

Parking and access are free. Camping is prohibited except at the Green Mountain Club cabins and shelters. The Greenwall shelter is located on the Greenwall Spur, 0.5 mile north of the Keewaydin Trail and Long Trail junction.

Maps

For a map of hiking trails, refer to map 6 in the *Map and Guide to the Appalachian Trail in New Hampshire/Vermont,* an eight-map set and guidebook available for $19.95 ($14.95 for the maps alone) from the Appalachian Trail Conference. Or get the waterproof *End-to-End Map of the Long Trail,* available for $8.95 from the Green Mountain Club. For a topographic area map, request Wallingford from USGS Map Sales, Federal Center, Box 25286,

Denver, CO 80225, 888/ASK-USGS (888/275-8747), website: http://mapping.usgs.gov.

Directions

From Route 140, 4.1 miles west of the junction of Routes 140 and 155 in East Wallingford and 2.1 miles east of the junction of 140 and U.S. 7 in Wallingford, turn south onto the dirt Sugar Hill Road. Drive 0.1 mile and turn right onto the dirt USFS Road 52 at a sign for the White Rocks Picnic Area. Continue 0.5 mile to the White Rocks Recreation Area.

Contact

Green Mountain National Forest Supervisor, 231 North Main Street, Rutland, VT 05701, 802/747-6700, fax 802/747-6766, website: www.fs.fed.us/r9/gmfl. Green Mountain Club Inc., 4711 Waterbury-Stowe Road, Waterbury Center, VT 05677, 802/244-7037, website: www.greenmountainclub.org. Appalachian Trail Conference, 799 Washington Street, P.O. Box 807, Harpers Ferry, WV 25425-0807, 304/535-6331, website: www.appalachiantrail.org.

27 THE LONG TRAIL: USFS ROAD 10 TO ROUTE 140

in the Green Mountain National Forest between Danby and Wallingford

Total distance: 9 miles one-way   **Hiking time:** 5.5 hours

Difficulty: 6   **Rating:** 7

The highlights of this fairly easy and relatively flat nine-mile stretch of the Long Trail/Appalachian Trail are Little Rock Pond and the view from White Rocks Cliff (see previous listing). From the parking area on USFS Road 10, cross the road onto the white-blazed Long Trail northbound. The trail follows Little Black Brook, passing the Lula Tye shelter at 1.8 miles and reaching Little Rock Pond, a small mountain tarn, at two miles. A popular destination with hikers, the pond sits tucked beneath a low ridge; there's a nice view across the pond where the Long Trail first reaches it at its southeast corner. Following the pond's east shore, the Long Trail reaches the short side path to Little Rock Pond shelter 0.1 mile beyond the pond, at 2.5 miles into this hike. The trail then climbs gently for 3.9 miles to a blue-blazed side path on the left that leads steeply downhill for 0.2 mile to White Rocks Cliff, with good views of the valley south of Wallingford. Continuing north, you reach a new section of the Long Trail, where it was rerouted in September 1999 in order to avoid wet areas and to reduce the amount of hiking on roadway. Turn left onto the new Long Trail, which coincides briefly with the Keewaydin Trail; the old Long Trail leading to the right has been renamed Greenwall Spur, and it leads 0.5 mile to the Greenwall shelter, dead-ending there. The Long Trail now follows the Keewaydin Trail a short distance, then swings right, crosses Bully Brook, crosses Sugar Hill Road, and reaches Route 140 about 0.75 mile west of the former trail crossing.

User Groups

Hikers, snowshoers, and dogs. Dogs must be leashed. No wheelchair facilities. This trail is not suitable for skis. Bikes, horses, and hunting are prohibited.

Access and Fees

Parking and access are free. USFS Road 10 is not maintained in winter. No-trace camping is permitted within the Green Mountain National Forest, except at Little Rock Pond, where camping within 200 feet of shore is allowed at designated campsites only. From late May to late October, a Green Mountain Club caretaker is on duty and a nightly fee of $6 per person is collected to stay at the Little Rock Pond and Lula Tye shelters and campsites. From USFS Road 10, the Lula Tye shelter is 1.8 miles north, the Little Rock Pond tenting area two miles north, the Little Rock Pond shelter 2.5 miles, and the Greenwall shelter 7.2 miles.

Maps

For a map of hiking trails, refer to map 6 in the *Map and Guide to the Appalachian Trail in New Hampshire/Vermont,* an eight-map set and guidebook available for $19.95 ($14.95 for the maps alone) from the Appalachian Trail Conference. Or get the waterproof *End-to-End Map of the Long Trail,* available for $8.95 from the Green Mountain Club. For topographic area maps, request Danby and Wallingford from USGS Map Sales, Federal Center, Box 25286, Denver, CO 80225, 888/ASK-USGS (888/275-8747), website: http://mapping.usgs.gov.

Directions

You need to shuttle two vehicles for this one-way traverse. To hike south to north, as described here, leave one vehicle where the Long Trail/Appalachian Trail crosses Route 140, about 2.8 miles east of U.S. 7 in Wallingford and about 3.7 miles west of the junction of Routes 140, 155, and 103 in East Wallingford. This hike begins at the parking lot on USFS Road 10 at Big Black Branch, 3.5 miles west of U.S. 7 in Danby and 13.6 miles north of Route 11 in Peru.

Contact

Green Mountain National Forest Supervisor, 231 North Main Street, Rutland, VT 05701, 802/747-6700, fax 802/747-6766, website: www.fs.fed.us/r9/gmfl. Green Mountain Club Inc., 4711 Waterbury-Stowe Road, Waterbury Center, VT 05677, 802/244-7037, website: www.greenmountainclub.org. Appalachian Trail Conference, 799 Washington Street, P.O. Box 807, Harpers Ferry, WV 25425-0807, 304/535-6331, website: www.appalachiantrail.org.

28 BIG BRANCH WILDERNESS

in the Green Mountain National Forest east of Danby

Total distance: 14 miles round-trip   **Hiking time:** 8.5 hours/1–2 days

Difficulty: 6   **Rating:** 9

I pulled this hike out of the full segment of the Long Trail described in the Long Trail: Route 11/30 to USFS Road 10 hike to highlight a trail section I particularly enjoy, from the roaring, rock-strewn bed of the Big Branch and placid Griffith Lake to the craggy heights of Baker Peak. This full trek is a fairly easy, 14-mile, out-and-back hike on the Long Trail from USFS Road 10 to Griffith Lake, which could be done in a day but is better spread over two days to enjoy the scenery. But I could also envision going no farther than any of the shelters along the way—even staying at the Big Branch shelter, a mere 1.3 miles into this hike, and hanging out by the river all day. Along the Big Branch are deep holes for fishing native brook and rainbow trout. The cumulative elevation gained hiking all the way to Griffith Lake and back is about 1,500 feet.

From the parking lot on USFS Road 10, walk east on the road for 0.1 mile and turn right, entering the woods on the white-blazed Long Trail southbound, which coincides here with the Appalachian Trail. It's an easy hike to the Big Branch stream and shelter. The trail parallels the stream for 0.1 mile, turns right and crosses it on a suspension bridge, then swings immediately left to follow the stream for another 0.1 mile before turning right, away from the stream. Following an old woods road over flat terrain, the Long Trail reaches the Lost Pond shelter via a short side path at three miles into this hike. The hiking remains relatively easy all the way to Baker Peak's open summit at five miles, where there is a wide view west toward the valley around the town of Danby and to Dorset Peak across the valley. Descending west off Baker Peak along a rock ridge for 0.1 mile, the Long Trail swings sharply left at a junction with the Baker Peak Trail. It then descends at a gentle angle to the Griffith Lake east shore and the campsite there at seven miles. Nearby, the Old Job Trail departs east and the Lake Trail departs west. This hike backtracks on the Long Trail to the road.

Special note: There are a couple of options to this hike. A one- or two-day, one-way traverse of eight miles begins at USFS Road 10 and descends from Baker Peak via the Baker Peak and Lake Trails. For a 13.7-mile loop of one or two days, hike the Long Trail south from USFS Road 10 to Griffith Lake and then loop back to the Big Branch suspension bridge on the Old Job Trail.

User Groups

Hikers and dogs. Dogs must be leashed. No wheelchair facilities. The trailhead is not accessible by road in winter for skiing or snowshoeing. Bikes, horses, and hunting are prohibited.

Access and Fees

Parking and access are free. USFS Road 10 is not maintained during the winter. No-trace camping is permitted within the Green Mountain National Forest, except at Griffith Lake, where camping within 200 feet of shore is restricted to designated sites. The Griffith Lake campsite is on the Long Trail, seven miles south of USFS Road 10. The Peru Peak shelter lies 0.7 mile farther south. From Memorial Day weekend to Labor Day, a Green Mountain Club caretaker is on duty and a nightly fee of $6 per person is collected to stay at both sites. The Big Branch shelter is on the Long Trail, 1.3 miles south of USFS Road 10, and the Lost Pond shelter is three miles south of the road.

Maps

For a map of hiking trails, refer to map 7 in the *Map and Guide to the Appalachian Trail in New Hampshire/Vermont,* an eight-map set and guidebook available for $19.95 ($14.95 for the maps alone) from the Appalachian Trail Conference. Or get the waterproof *End-to-End Map of the Long Trail,* available for $8.95 from the Green Mountain Club. For a topographic area map, request Danby from USGS Map Sales, Federal Center, Box 25286, Denver, CO 80225, 888/ASK-USGS (888/275-8747), website: http://mapping.usgs.gov.

Directions

Drive to the parking lot on USFS Road 10 at Big Black Branch, 3.5 miles west of U.S. 7 in Danby and 13.6 miles north of Route

11 in Peru. To finish this hike on the Baker Peak and Lake Trail, as described in the special note above, you must leave a vehicle at the start of the Lake Trail; from the crossroads in Danby, drive south on U.S. 7 for 2.1 miles and turn left onto Town Route 5. Drive 0.5 mile to parking on the left.

Contact

Green Mountain National Forest Supervisor, 231 North Main Street, Rutland, VT 05701, 802/747-6700, fax 802/747-6766, website: www.fs.fed.us/r9/gmfl. Green Mountain Club Inc., 4711 Waterbury-Stowe Road, Waterbury Center, VT 05677, 802/244-7037, website: www.greenmountainclub.org. Appalachian Trail Conference, 799 Washington Street, P.O. Box 807, Harpers Ferry, WV 25425-0807, 304/535-6331, website: www.appalachiantrail.org.

29 GRIFFITH LAKE AND BAKER PEAK

in the Green Mountain National Forest southeast of Danby

Total distance: 8.5 miles round-trip   **Hiking time:** 6 hours

Difficulty: 8   **Rating:** 9

Baker Peak, though just 2,850 feet high, thrusts a rocky spine above the trees for great views of the valley around the little town of Danby. And Griffith Lake is one of several scenic ponds and lakes along the Long Trail. This 8.5-mile loop incorporates both places and involves about 2,000 feet of climbing.

From the parking area, follow the Lake Trail. It ascends very gently at first, then steeply for two miles. Where the Baker Peak Trail bears left, stay to the right on the Lake Trail. It nearly levels off again before reaching the Long Trail—which coincides here with the Appalachian Trail—at 3.5 miles from the trailhead. Turning right (south), walk the Long Trail for 0.1 mile to the Griffith Lake camping area and access views of the lake. Spin around and hike north on the Long Trail for 1.8 relatively easy miles to the Baker Peak Trail junction. Here, turn right with the Long Trail and scramble up the long rock ridge protruding from the earth for 0.1 mile to the open Baker Peak summit. Then backtrack, descending the Baker Peak Trail, past the Quarry View overlook, for a mile to the Lake Trail. Turn right (west) and descend another two miles to the parking area.

User Groups

Hikers, snowshoers, and dogs. Dogs must be leashed. No wheelchair facilities. This trail is not suitable for skis. Bikes, horses, and hunting are prohibited.

Access and Fees

Parking and access are free. Camping is prohibited except at the Green Mountain Club cabins and shelters. The Griffith Lake camping area, with tent sites, is located 0.1 mile south of the Lake and Long Trails junction. From Memorial Day weekend to Labor Day, a Green Mountain Club caretaker is on duty and a nightly fee of $6 per person is collected.

Maps

For a map of hiking trails, refer to map 7 in the *Map and Guide to the Appalachian Trail in New Hampshire/Vermont,* an eight-map set and guidebook available for $19.95 ($14.95 for the maps alone) from the Appalachian Trail Conference. Or get the waterproof *End-to-End Map of the Long Trail,* available for $8.95 from the Green Mountain Club. For a topographic area map, request Danby from USGS Map Sales, Federal Center, Box 25286, Denver, CO 80225, 888/ASK-USGS (888/275-8747), website: http://mapping.usgs.gov.

Directions

From the crossroads in Danby, drive south on U.S. 7 for 2.1 miles and turn left onto Town Route 5. Drive 0.5 mile to parking on the left for the Lake Trail.

Contact

Green Mountain National Forest Supervisor, 231 North Main Street, Rutland, VT 05701, 802/747-6700, fax 802/747-6766, website: www.fs.fed.us/r9/gmfl. Green Mountain Club Inc., 4711 Waterbury-Stowe Road, Waterbury Center, VT 05677, 802/244-7037, website: www.greenmountainclub.org. Appalachian Trail Conference, 799 Washington Street, P.O. Box 807, Harpers Ferry, WV 25425-0807, 304/535-6331, website: www.appalachiantrail.org.

30 THE LONG TRAIL: ROUTE 11/30 TO USFS ROAD 10

in the Green Mountain National Forest east of Danby

Total distance: 17.3 miles one-way   **Hiking time:** 2 days

Difficulty: 8   **Rating:** 9

I have a personal bias regarding the mountains—I prefer hikes with good views and those that inspire a sense of solitude. Those two features are not always mutually compatible in New England. But when I hiked much of the Long Trail in October 1996, this fairly scenic stretch gave me just that sort of experience. Timing no doubt helped; I started my trip after the leaves had fallen off the trees. One of my favorite moments was standing alone on the Styles Peak summit at sunset. Another was sitting on big rocks beside the roaring, clear waters of the Big Branch, with no one around. I'd recommend this 17.3-mile stretch for a moderate, two-day backpacking trip. The cumulative elevation gain is nearly 3,000 feet, but spread over more than 17 miles.

From the parking lot on Route 11/30, follow the white blazes of the Long Trail northbound, which here coincides with the Appalachian Trail. Watch closely for the blazes; many unmarked trails cross the Long Trail on this side of Bromley. At 0.8 mile into this hike, a spur trail leads 150 feet to the right to the Bromley tenting area. Two miles from the road, the Long Trail grows steeper, and at 2.6 miles it emerges from the woods onto a wide ski trail. Hike up the ski trail 0.2 mile to the mountain's summit, where there are ski area buildings. To the right are an observation deck—which offers views in every direction—and the warming hut. The Long Trail swings left from the ski trail just before a chairlift and descends a steep, rocky section. At 3.3 miles (0.5 mile beyond the summit), the Long Trail climbs over the rugged, wooded north summit of Bromley and then descends to cross USFS Road 21 in Mad Tom Notch at 5.3 miles. There is a water pump at the roadside that may not be working. Continuing north, the Long Trail makes a steady, though not difficult, ascent of nearly 1,000 feet in elevation to the 3,394-foot Styles Peak summit, at 6.7 miles. Although I mentioned enjoying the sunset from this summit, I couldn't actually see the sunset, but the wide view south and west showed me long shadows across the land, and Styles's own pyramidal shadow.

Following the ridge north, the Long Trail dips slightly and then ascends slightly to the wooded Peru Peak summit (3,429 feet) at 8.4 miles, where a side path leads 75 feet right to a largely obscured view eastward. Descending steeply, the trail reaches the Peru Peak shelter at 9.7 miles, with a good stream nearby. The Long Trail crosses the stream on a wooden bridge and continues a flat 0.7 mile to Griffith Lake at 10.4 miles, where there are tent sites. The Old Job Trail leaves right (east), swinging north to loop 5.3 miles back to the Long Trail at a point 0.1 mile east of the Big Branch suspension bridge. The Lake Trail departs left (west) at 10.5 miles, descending 3.5 miles to Town Route 5 in Danby (0.5 mile from U.S. 7).

The Long Trail continues north over easy terrain and then climbs to a junction, at 12.2 miles, with the Baker Peak Trail (which descends west for 2.9 miles to Town Route 5 via the Lake Trail). Turn right with the Long Trail and scramble up a spine of exposed rock for 0.1 mile to the open summit of 2,850-foot Baker Peak, with great views of the valley around the little town of Danby. The trail then reenters the forest and traverses fairly easy terrain, reaching and following an old woods road to a junction, at 14.3 miles, with a short side path leading left to the Lost Pond shelter.

Continuing on the woods road, the Long Trail reaches the Big Branch at 15.8 miles, swings left along it for 0.1 mile, and then crosses the river on a suspension bridge. The trail swings left again, following the boulder-choked river to the Big Branch shelter at 16 miles. Easy hiking for another 1.2 miles brings you to USFS Road 10. Turn left and walk the road for 0.1 mile to the parking lot at this hike's north end.

User Groups

Hikers and dogs. Dogs must be leashed. No wheelchair facilities. This trail is not suitable for skis. The north end of this trail is not accessible by road in winter for snowshoeing. Bikes, horses, and hunting are prohibited.

Access and Fees

Parking and access are free. USFS Road 10 is not maintained

during the winter. No-trace camping is permitted within the Green Mountain National Forest, except at Griffith Lake, where camping within 200 feet of shore is restricted to designated sites. Backpackers can stay overnight in the warming hut on Bromley Mountain's summit, beside the observation deck; there is no water source. The Bromley tenting area is 0.7 mile north of Route 11/30, reached via a short spur trail off the Long Trail. The Peru Peak shelter sits beside the Long Trail at 9.8 miles, the Griffith Lake campsite at 10.3 miles, the Lost Pond shelter at 14.5 miles, and the Big Branch shelter at 16.2 miles (the last 1.3 miles south of the parking lot on USFS Road 10). The Mad Tom shelter was removed in 1997. From Memorial Day weekend to Labor Day, a Green Mountain Club caretaker is on duty, and a nightly fee of $6 per person is collected to stay at the Peru Peak shelter and the Griffith Lake campsite.

Maps

For a map of hiking trails, refer to map 7 in the *Map and Guide to the Appalachian Trail in New Hampshire/Vermont,* an eight-map set and guidebook available for $19.95 ($14.95 for the maps alone) from the Appalachian Trail Conference. Or get the water-proof *End-to-End Map of the Long Trail,* available for $8.95 from the Green Mountain Club. For topographic area maps, request Peru and Danby from USGS Map Sales, Federal Center, Box 25286, Denver, CO 80225, 888/ASK-USGS (888/275-8747), web-site: http://mapping.usgs.gov.

Directions

You need to shuttle two vehicles for this one-way traverse. To hike south to north, as described here, leave one vehicle in the parking lot on USFS Road 10 at Big Black Branch, 3.5 miles west of U.S. 7 in Danby and 13.6 miles north of Route 11 in Peru. Drive to the parking lot on the north side of Route 11/30, six miles east of Manchester Center and 4.4 miles west of Peru.

Contact

Green Mountain National Forest Supervisor, 231 North Main Street, Rutland, VT 05701, 802/747-6700, fax 802/747-6766, website: www.fs.fed.us/r9/gmfl. Green Mountain Club Inc.,

31 STYLES PEAK

in the Peru Peak Wilderness in the Green Mountain
National Forest west of Peru

Total distance: 2.8 miles round-trip | **Hiking time:** 2 hours

Difficulty: 4 | **Rating:** 8

Styles Peak, 3,394 feet high, has a small crag of a summit that affords views to the east and south of the southern Green Mountains and the rumpled landscape of southeastern Vermont and southwestern New Hampshire. This quiet spot is a great place to catch the sunrise, and with just 1.4 miles to hike nearly 1,000 feet uphill to reach the summit, getting here before dawn is a reasonable objective.

From the parking area, walk east a few steps on the road to the junction with the Long Trail and turn left (north). After passing a water pump (which may not be working), follow the white-blazed Long Trail, which coincides here with the Appalachian Trail as it climbs steadily and then steeply to the open rocks atop Styles Peak. Return the way you came.

User Groups

Hikers, snowshoers, and dogs. Dogs must be leashed. No wheelchair facilities. Bikes, horses, and hunting are prohibited.

Access and Fees

Parking and access are free. USFS Road 21 is maintained in winter only to a point about 2.5 miles from the Long Trail. No-trace camping is permitted within the Green Mountain National Forest. The Peru Peak shelter is on the Long Trail, 4.4 miles north of USFS Road 21 and three miles north of the Styles Peak summit. From Memorial Day weekend to Labor Day, a Green Mountain Club caretaker is on duty and collects a nightly fee of $6 per person.

Maps

For a trail map, see map 7 in the *Map and Guide to the Appalachian Trail in New Hampshire/Vermont,* an eight-map set and guidebook available for $19.95 ($14.95 for the maps alone) from the Appalachian Trail Conference. Or get the waterproof *End-to-*

End Map of the Long Trail, available for $8.95 from the Green Mountain Club. For a topographic area map, request Peru from USGS Map Sales, Federal Center, Box 25286, Denver, CO 80225, 888/ASK-USGS (888/275-8747), website: http://mapping.usgs.gov.

Directions
Drive to the parking area on USFS Road 21, immediately west of the height of land in Mad Tom Notch and the Long Trail crossing, and 4.3 miles west of Route 11 in Peru.

Contact
Green Mountain National Forest Supervisor, 231 North Main Street, Rutland, VT 05701, 802/747-6700, fax 802/747-6766, website: www.fs.fed.us/r9/gmfl. Green Mountain Club Inc., 4711 Waterbury-Stowe Road, Waterbury Center, VT 05677, 802/244-7037, website: www.greenmountainclub.org. Appalachian Trail Conference, 799 Washington Street, P.O. Box 807, Harpers Ferry, WV 25425-0807, 304/535-6331, website: www.appalachiantrail.org.

32 BROMLEY MOUNTAIN FROM MAD TOM NOTCH

in the Green Mountain National Forest west of Peru

Total distance: 5 miles round-trip **Hiking time:** 3.5 hours

Difficulty: 6 **Rating:** 9

This five-mile route from the north up 3,260-foot Bromley Mountain is a bit more wild and less trammeled than taking the Long Trail from the south (see the previous listing for more information). A ski area in winter, Bromley offers some of the better views along the southern Long Trail from its summit observation deck. This hike climbs about 800 feet.

From the parking lot, walk east on the road for a short stretch, then turn right and follow the white blazes of the Long Trail southbound, which here coincides with the Appalachian Trail. The trail ascends easily at first and then climbs more steeply, over rocky terrain, to Bromley's wooded north summit at two miles. After dipping slightly, it climbs to the open summit of Bromley Mountain, 2.5 miles from the road. Cross the clearing to the observation deck and warming hut. Descend the same way you came.

User Groups

Hikers and dogs. Dogs must be leashed. No wheelchair facilities. This trail may be difficult to snowshoe and is not suitable for skis. Bikes, horses, and hunting are prohibited.

Access and Fees

Parking and access are free. USFS Road 21 is maintained in winter only to a point about 2.5 miles from the Long Trail. No-trace camping is permitted within the Green Mountain National Forest. Backpackers can stay overnight in the warming hut on Bromley's summit, beside the observation deck; there is no water source.

Maps

For a map of hiking trails, refer to map 7 in the *Map and Guide to the Appalachian Trail in New Hampshire/Vermont,* an eight-map set and guidebook available for $19.95 ($14.95 for the maps alone) from the Appalachian Trail Conference. Or get the water-proof *End-to-End Map of the Long Trail,* available for $8.95 from the Green Mountain Club. For a topographic area map, request Peru from USGS Map Sales, Federal Center, Box 25286, Denver, CO 80225, 888/ASK-USGS (888/275-8747), website: http://mapping.usgs.gov.

Directions
Drive to the parking area on USFS Road 21, immediately west of the height of land in Mad Tom Notch and the Long Trail crossing, and 4.3 miles west of Route 11 in Peru.

Contact
Green Mountain National Forest Supervisor, 231 North Main Street, Rutland, VT 05701, 802/747-6700, fax 802/747-6766, website: www.fs.fed.us/r9/gmfl. Green Mountain Club Inc., 4711 Waterbury-Stowe Road, Waterbury Center, VT 05677, 802/244-7037, fax 802/244-5867, website: www.greenmountainclub.org. Appalachian Trail Conference, 799 Washington Street, P.O. Box 807, Harpers Ferry, WV 25425-0807, 304/535-6331, website: www.appalachiantrail.org.

33 BROMLEY MOUNTAIN FROM ROUTE 11/30

in the Green Mountain National Forest between Peru and Manchester Center

Total distance: 5.6 miles round-trip

Hiking time: 3.5 hours

Difficulty: 6

Rating: 9

Bromley Mountain, a ski area in winter, offers some of the better views along the southern Long Trail from the observation deck on its 3,260-foot summit. This 5.6-mile route up Bromley is a popular hike and suffers from erosion and muddy ground in many places. It ascends 1,460 feet.

From the parking lot, follow the white blazes of the Long Trail northbound, which here coincides with the Appalachian Trail. Watch closely for the blazes; numerous unmarked trails cross the Long Trail on this side of Bromley. At two miles into this hike you reach the Bromley shelter, where there's a lean-to that sleeps 12 and four tent platforms. Beyond it, the Long Trail grows steeper, and at 2.6 miles it emerges from the woods onto a wide ski trail. Hike up the ski trail 0.2 mile to the mountain's summit, where there are ski area buildings. Turn right and walk 100 feet to the observation deck. The views extend in every direction. Stratton Mountain looms prominently to the south. Beside the tower is the warming hut. Descend the way you came.

User Groups

Hikers, snowshoers, and dogs. Dogs must be leashed. No wheelchair facilities. This trail is not suitable for skis. Bikes, horses, and hunting are prohibited.

Access and Fees

Parking and access are free. No-trace camping is permitted within the Green Mountain National Forest. The Bromley shelter and tent platforms are two miles north of Route 11/30. Backpackers can stay overnight in the warming hut on Bromley's summit, beside the observation deck; there is no water source.

Maps

For a map of hiking trails, refer to map 7 in the *Map and Guide to the Appalachian Trail in New Hampshire/Vermont,* an eight-map set and guidebook available for $19.95 ($14.95 for the maps alone) from the Appalachian Trail Conference. Or get the waterproof *End-to-End Map of the Long Trail,* available for $8.95 from the Green Mountain Club. For a topographic area map, request Peru from USGS Map Sales, Federal Center, Box 25286, Denver, CO 80225, 888/ASK-USGS (888/275-8747), website: http://mapping.usgs.gov.

Directions

Drive to the parking lot on the north side of Route 11/30, six miles east of Manchester Center and 4.4 miles west of Peru.

Contact

Green Mountain National Forest Supervisor, 231 North Main Street, Rutland, VT 05701, 802/747-6700, fax 802/747-6766, website: www.fs.fed.us/r9/gmfl. Green Mountain Club Inc., 4711 Waterbury-Stowe Road, Waterbury Center, VT 05677, 802/244-7037, website: www.greenmountainclub.org. Appalachian Trail Conference, 799 Washington Street, P.O. Box 807, Harpers Ferry, WV 25425-0807, 304/535-6331, website: www.appalachiantrail.org.

34 SPRUCE PEAK

in the Green Mountain National Forest south of Peru

Total distance: 4.4 miles round-trip   **Hiking time:** 2.5 hours

Difficulty: 4   **Rating:** 8

This fairly easy hike of 4.4 miles takes you up to Spruce Peak, at 2,040 feet no more than a small bump along a wooded Green Mountain ridge, but a spot with a couple of good views west to the valley at Manchester Center and out to the Taconic Range. On my trip, I happened to time this hike perfectly, enjoying the view on a cloudless Indian summer day in October when the foliage in the valley below was at its peak.

From the parking area, cross Route 11/30 and follow the white blazes of the Long Trail southbound into the woods. The hiking is mostly easy, climbing only a few hundred feet in elevation, with the trail passing through an area of moss-covered boulders and rocks. At 2.2 miles from the road, turn right (west) onto a side path that leads about 300 feet to the Spruce Peak summit. There is a limited view west at the actual summit, but just below the summit, a few steps off the path, is a better view. Return the way you came.

User Groups

Hikers, snowshoers, and dogs. Dogs must be leashed. No wheelchair facilities. Bikes, horses, and hunting are prohibited.

Access and Fees

Parking and access are free. No-trace camping is permitted within the Green Mountain National Forest. The Spruce Peak shelter is 0.1 mile down a side path off the Long Trail, 2.7 miles south of Route 11/30 and 0.5 mile south of the side path to Spruce Peak.

Maps

For a map of hiking trails, refer to map 7 in the *Map and Guide to the Appalachian Trail in New Hampshire/Vermont,* an eight-map set and guidebook available for $19.95 ($14.95 for the maps alone) from the Appalachian Trail Conference. Or get the waterproof *End-to-End Map of the Long Trail,* available for $8.95 from the Green Mountain Club. For a topographic area map, request Peru from USGS Map Sales, Federal Center, Box 25286, Denver, CO 80225, 888/ASK-USGS (888/275-8747), website: http://mapping.usgs.gov.

Directions
Drive to the parking lot on the north side of Route 11/30, six miles east of Manchester Center and 4.4 miles west of Peru.

Contact
Green Mountain National Forest Supervisor, 231 North Main Street, Rutland, VT 05701, 802/747-6700, fax 802/747-6766, website: www.fs.fed.us/r9/gmfl. Green Mountain Club Inc., 4711 Waterbury-Stowe Road, Waterbury Center, VT 05677, 802/244-7037, website: www.greenmountainclub.org. Appalachian Trail Conference, 799 Washington Street, P.O. Box 807, Harpers Ferry, WV 25425-0807, 304/535-6331, website: www.appalachiantrail.org.

35 THE LONG TRAIL: ARLINGTON–WEST WARDSBORO ROAD TO ROUTE 11/30

in the Green Mountain National Forest between Stratton and Peru

Total distance: 16.3 miles one-way **Hiking time:** 11 hours/1–2 days

Difficulty: 8 **Rating:** 9

The highlights of this 16.3-mile traverse of the Long Trail's southern stretch are the 360-degree view from the observation tower on 3,936-foot Stratton Mountain, and beautiful Stratton Pond. But you also get a view from Spruce Peak, and the northern part of this trek will feel considerably more secluded than Stratton Pond or Stratton Mountain. The cumulative elevation gain is more than 2,500 feet, most of that involved in the 1,800-foot climb up Stratton Mountain.

From the parking area, head north on the white-blazed Long Trail (which coincides here with the Appalachian Trail). It rises gently through muddy areas, growing progressively steeper—and passing one outlook south—over the 3.4-mile climb to Stratton's summit. A Green Mountain Club caretaker cabin is located on the edge of the summit clearing, and a caretaker is on duty during the hiking season (late spring to fall) to answer questions and assist hikers. After climbing the observation tower (see Stratton Mountain and Stratton Pond listing for a description of the view from the tower), continue north on the Long Trail, descending for 2.6 miles to Willis Ross Clearing on the east shore of Stratton Pond, the largest water body and one of the busiest spots on the Long Trail. The Lye Brook Trail leads left while the Long Trail swings right, passing a junction with the North Shore Trail within 0.1 mile. The Long Trail contours, for easy hiking, to the Winhall River at 7.9 miles into this hike; the river is crossed on a bridge, and the trail enters the Lye Brook Wilderness.

At 10.3 miles, the Branch Pond Trail leads left (west) into the Lye Brook Wilderness to the William B. Douglas shelter. Crossing a brook, the Long Trail turns left and follows a wide logging road. At 11.4 miles, an unmarked side path leads about 200 feet to Prospect Rock, with a good view of Downer Glen. The Long

Trail turns right (northeast) off the road and climbs steadily before descending again to a side path, at 13.6 miles, leading 0.1 mile to the Spruce Peak cabin. After more easy hiking, at 14.1 miles, a side path leads about 300 feet left to the Spruce Peak summit, where there is a limited view west. But just below the summit is a better view of the valley and the Taconic Mountains. Continuing north, the Long Trail crosses easy ground for 2.2 miles, passing through an area of interesting, moss-covered boulders, to reach Routes 11/30 at 16.3 miles. Cross the highway to the parking lot.

User Groups

Hikers and dogs. Dogs must be leashed. No wheelchair facilities. This trail is not suitable for skis. The south end of this trail is not accessible by road in winter for snowshoeing. Bikes, horses, and hunting are prohibited.

Access and Fees

Parking and access are free. The Arlington–West Wardsboro Road is not maintained in winter. No-trace camping is permitted within the Green Mountain National Forest, except at Stratton Pond, where camping is restricted to the North Shore tenting area, which lies 0.5 mile down the North Shore Trail from its junction with the Long Trail, 0.1 mile north of Willis Ross Clearing; and the new Stratton Pond shelter, located 100 yards down the Stratton Pond Trail from its junction with the Long Trail/Appalachian Trail. From Memorial Day weekend to Columbus Day, a Green Mountain Club caretaker is on duty, and a nightly fee of $6 per person is collected to stay at the Stratton Pond shelter and the North Shore tenting area. Two Green Mountain Club shelters on Stratton Pond—Vondell shelter and Bigelow shelter—were removed in the fall of 2000 and 1997, respectively. Camping is prohibited on the upper slopes of Stratton Mountain, which is privately owned. The Williams B. Douglas shelter lies 0.5 mile south of the Long Trail on the Branch Pond Trail, 10.3 miles north of the Arlington–West Wardsboro Road. The Spruce Peak shelter lies 0.1 mile down a side path off the Long Trail, at 13.6 miles into this hike.

Maps

For a map of hiking trails, refer to map 7 in the *Map and Guide to the Appalachian Trail in New Hampshire/Vermont,* an eight-map set and guidebook available for $19.95 ($14.95 for the maps alone) from the Appalachian Trail Conference. Or get the waterproof *End-to-End Map of the Long Trail,* available for $8.95 from the Green Mountain Club. For topographic area maps, request Stratton Mountain, Manchester, and Peru from USGS Map Sales, Federal Center, Box 25286, Denver, CO 80225, 888/ASK-USGS (888/275-8747), website: http://mapping.usgs.gov.

Directions

You need to shuttle two vehicles for this one-way traverse. To hike south to north, as described here, leave one vehicle in the parking lot on the north side of Route 11/30, six miles east of Manchester Center and 4.4 miles west of Peru. Then drive to the large parking area on the Arlington–West Wardsboro Road, 13.3 miles east of U.S. 7 in Arlington and eight miles west of Route 100 in West Wardsboro.

Contact

Green Mountain National Forest Supervisor, 231 North Main Street, Rutland, VT 05701, 802/747-6700, fax 802/747-6766, website: www.fs.fed.us/r9/gmfl. Green Mountain Club Inc., 4711 Waterbury-Stowe Road, Waterbury Center, VT 05677, 802/244-7037, website: www.greenmountainclub.org. Appalachian Trail Conference, 799 Washington Street, P.O. Box 807, Harpers Ferry, WV 25425-0807, 304/535-6331, website: www.appalachiantrail.org.

36 STRATTON MOUNTAIN AND STRATTON POND

in the Green Mountain National Forest between
Arlington and West Wardsboro

Total distance: 11 miles round-trip   **Hiking time:** 7 hours

Difficulty: 8   **Rating:** 10

From the observation tower atop Stratton Mountain, you get one of the most sweeping panoramas on the Long Trail. And merely climbing the tower will be an adventure for children, as well as adults not accustomed to heights. This 11-mile hike climbs about 1,500 feet. For a shorter hike—though with just as much climbing—you can make a 6.8-mile round-trip on the Long Trail to the 3,936-foot Stratton summit and return the same way.

From the parking area, follow the white-blazed Long Trail north (which coincides here with the Appalachian Trail). It rises steadily, through muddy areas at the lower elevations, and passes one outlook south in the 3.4-mile climb—the last stretch of which grows steeper. On the 3,936-foot summit is the Green Mountain Club's caretaker cabin, and a caretaker is on duty during the hiking season (late spring to fall) to answer questions and assist hikers. Climb the fire tower, where the views take in Somerset Reservoir and Mount Greylock to the south, the Taconic Range to the west, Mount Ascutney to the northeast, and Mount Monadnock to the southeast.

Return the same way, or make an 11-mile loop by continuing north on the Long Trail, descending for 2.6 miles to beautiful Stratton Pond, the largest body of water and one of the busiest areas on the Long Trail. The Long Trail reaches the east shore of Stratton Pond at Willis Ross Clearing. From here, a loop of about 1.5 miles around the pond is possible, taking the Lye Brook Trail along the south shore, and the North Shore Trail back to the Long Trail, 0.1 mile north of Willis Ross Clearing; this distance is not included in this hike's mileage. From the clearing, backtrack 0.1 mile south on the Long Trail, turn right onto the Stratton Pond Trail, and follow it for an easy 3.8 miles back to the Arlington–West Wardsboro Road. Turn left (east) and walk the road 1.1 miles back to the parking area.

User Groups

Hikers and dogs. Dogs must be leashed. No wheelchair facilities. This trail is not suitable for skis. The trailhead is not accessible by road in winter for snowshoeing. Bikes, horses, and hunting are prohibited.

Access and Fees

Parking and access are free. The Arlington–West Wardsboro Road is not maintained in winter. No-trace camping is permitted within the Green Mountain National Forest, except at Stratton Pond, where camping is restricted to the North Shore tenting area, which lies 0.5 mile down the North Shore Trail from its junction with the Long Trail, 0.1 mile north of Willis Ross Clearing; and the new Stratton Pond shelter, located 100 yards down the Stratton Pond Trail from its junction with the Long Trail/Appalachian Trail. From Memorial Day weekend to Columbus Day, a Green Mountain Club caretaker is on duty, and a nightly fee of $6 per person is collected to stay at the Stratton shelter and the North Shore tenting area. Two Green Mountain Club shelters on Stratton Pond—Vondell shelter and Bigelow shelter—were removed in the fall of 2000 and in 1997, respectively. Camping is prohibited on the upper slopes of Stratton Mountain, which is privately owned.

Maps

For a map of hiking trails, refer to map 7 in the *Map and Guide to the Appalachian Trail in New Hampshire/Vermont,* an eight-map set and guidebook available for $19.95 ($14.95 for the maps alone) from the Appalachian Trail Conference. Or get the waterproof *End-to-End Map of the Long Trail,* available for $8.95 from the Green Mountain Club. For a topographic area map, request Stratton Mountain from USGS Map Sales, Federal Center, Box 25286, Denver, CO 80225, 888/ASK-USGS (888/275-8747), website: http://mapping.usgs.gov.

Directions

The hike begins from a large parking area on the Arlington–West Wardsboro Road, 13.3 miles east of U.S. 7 in Arlington and eight miles west of Route 100 in West Wardsboro.

Contact

Green Mountain National Forest Supervisor, 231 North Main Street, Rutland, VT 05701, 802/747-6700, fax 802/747-6766, website: www.fs.fed.us/r9/gmfl. Green Mountain Club Inc., 4711 Waterbury-Stowe Road, Waterbury Center, VT 05677, 802/244-7037, website: www.greenmountainclub.org. Appalachian Trail Conference, 799 Washington Street, P.O. Box 807, Harpers Ferry, WV 25425-0807, 304/535-6331, website: www.appalachiantrail.org.

37 THE LONG TRAIL: ROUTE 9 TO ARLINGTON–WEST WARDSBORO ROAD

in the Green Mountain National Forest between
Woodford and Stratton

Total distance: 22.3 miles one-way   **Hiking time:** 2–3 days

Difficulty: 6   **Rating:** 8

While much of this 22.3-mile stretch of the Long Trail/Appalachian Trail remains in the woods, it makes for a nice walk along a wooded ridge, on a relatively easy backpacking trip that can be done in two days without extreme effort. And there are a few breathtaking views, most particularly from the fire tower on the 3,748-foot Glastenbury Mountain summit, which offers one of the finest panoramas I've seen on the Long Trail. The cumulative elevation gain over the course of this hike exceeds 4,000 feet.

From the parking lot, follow the white blazes of the Long Trail northbound. The trail parallels City Stream briefly and then crosses it on a wooden bridge. Climbing steadily, the trail crosses an old woods road 0.2 mile from the highway and then passes between the twin halves of Split Rock, formerly one giant boulder, at 0.6 mile. At 1.5 miles, a side path leads right a short distance to the Nauheim shelter. Ascending north from the shelter, the trail crosses a power line atop Maple Hill at two miles, which affords a view toward Bennington. The trail then traverses the more level terrain of a wooded ridge and crosses Hell Hollow Brook, a reliable water source, on a bridge at three miles.

Passing through a stand of beech trees, the Long Trail reaches Little Pond Lookout at 5.7 miles, with a good view east, then Glastenbury Lookout at 7.4 miles, with its view of Glastenbury Mountain. The trail then ascends about 600 feet at a moderate angle to Goddard shelter, at 9.8 miles. From the shelter, it's a not-too-rigorous, 0.3-mile walk uphill on the Long Trail to the Glastenbury summit. From the fire tower, the 360-degree view encompasses the Berkshires—most prominently Mount Greylock—to the south, the Taconic Range to the west, Stratton Mountain to the north, and Somerset Reservoir to the east. Continuing north, the Long Trail descends about 500 feet in elevation and then follows a wooded ridge, with slight rises and dips, for about four miles, finally descending at a moderate angle to a side path on the right at 14 miles, which leads 0.1 mile to the Kid Gore shelter. About 0.1 mile farther north on the Long Trail, the other end of that side loop reaches the Long Trail near the Caughnawaga shelter. The Long Trail then goes through more slight ups and downs before reaching the Story Spring shelter, 18.7 miles north of Route 9 and 3.6 miles south of the Arlington–West Wardsboro Road. The Long Trail crosses USFS Road 71 at 20.3 miles, passes beaver ponds, traverses an area often wet and muddy, and then crosses Black Brook, a reliable water source, on a wooden bridge at 21.3 miles. Paralleling the east branch of the Deerfield River, the trail reaches the Arlington–West Wardsboro Road at 22.3 miles. Turn right (east) and walk 200 feet to the parking area.

User Groups

Hikers, snowshoers, and dogs. Dogs must be leashed. No wheelchair facilities. This trail is not suitable for skis. Bikes, horses, and hunting are prohibited.

Access and Fees

Parking and access are free. The Arlington–West Wardsboro Road is not maintained in winter. No-trace camping is permitted within the Green Mountain National Forest. The Green Mountain Club Melville Nauheim shelter is located 1.6 miles north of Route 9 on the Long Trail, the Goddard shelter at 10.1 miles, the Kid Gore shelter at 14.2 miles, the Caughnawaga shelter at 14.4 miles, and the Story Spring shelter at 19 miles (or 3.6 miles south of the Arlington–West Wardsboro Road).

Maps

For a map of hiking trails, refer to map 8 in the *Map and Guide to the Appalachian Trail in New Hampshire/Vermont,* an eight-map set and guidebook available for $19.95 ($14.95 for the maps alone) from the Appalachian Trail Conference. Or get the waterproof *End-to-End Map of the Long Trail,* available for $8.95 from the Green Mountain Club. For topographic area maps, request Woodford, Sunderland, and Stratton Mountain from USGS Map Sales, Federal Center, Box 25286, Denver, CO 80225, 888/ASK-USGS (888/275-8747), website: http://mapping.usgs.gov.

Directions

You need to shuttle two vehicles for this one-way traverse. To hike south to north, as described here, leave one vehicle in the roadside parking area where the Long Trail/Appalachian Trail crosses the Arlington–West Wardsboro Road, 13.3 miles east of U.S. 7 in Arlington and eight miles west of Route 100 in West Wardsboro. Then drive to the large parking lot at the Long Trail/Appalachian Trail crossing of Route 9, 5.2 miles east of Bennington and 2.8 miles west of Woodford.

Contact

Green Mountain National Forest Supervisor, 231 North Main Street, Rutland, VT 05701, 802/747-6700, fax 802/747-6766, website: www.fs.fed.us/r9/gmfl. Green Mountain Club Inc., 4711 Waterbury-Stowe Road, Waterbury Center, VT 05677, 802/244-7037, website: www.greenmountainclub.org. Appalachian Trail Conference, 799 Washington Street, P.O. Box 807, Harpers Ferry, WV 25425-0807, 304/535-6331, website: www.appalachiantrail.org.

38 GLASTENBURY MOUNTAIN

in the Green Mountain National Forest between
Bennington and Woodford

Total distance: 20.2 miles round-trip   **Hiking time:** 2 days

Difficulty: 8   **Rating:** 9

While much of the southern third of the Long Trail, which coincides with the Appalachian Trail, remains in the woods, the fire
tower on the 3,748-foot Glastenbury Mountain summit offers a
superb panorama of the gently rolling southern Green Mountains wilderness. Other views include the Berkshires, particularly
Mount Greylock, due south, the Taconic Range to the west,
Stratton Mountain to the north, and Somerset Reservoir to the
east. I stood up here one afternoon at the height of the fall foliage, and it turned out to be one of the finest views I had in my
lengthy Long Trail trek.

This 20.2-mile round-trip—which involves nearly 4,000 feet of
uphill—is best spread over two days, with an overnight stay at
the spacious Goddard shelter (or tenting in the area). Goddard,
which has a nice view south to Greylock, can be a popular place
on temperate weekends in summer and fall. See the trail notes
for the Long Trail: Route 9 to Arlington–West Wardsboro Road
(previous listing) for the description of this hike from Route 9 to
the Goddard shelter. At the shelter, leave your packs behind for
the 0.3-mile walk uphill on the Long Trail to the Glastenbury
summit and the fire tower. On the second day, you can return
the same way you came. Or to avoid backtracking, hike the
West Ridge Trail from Goddard shelter, a fairly easy route that
leads 7.7 miles to the Bald Mountain summit and a junction at
7.8 miles with the Bald Mountain Trail. Turn left on that trail
and descend 1.9 miles to a public road. Turning right on the
road, you reach Route 9 in 0.8 mile, 1.2 miles west of the parking lot where you began this hike.

User Groups

Hikers, snowshoers, and dogs. Dogs must be leashed. No wheelchair facilities. This trail is not suitable for skis. Bikes, horses,
and hunting are prohibited.

Access and Fees

Parking and access are free. No-trace camping is permitted within the Green Mountain National Forest. The Green Mountain Club Melville Nauheim shelter is located 1.6 miles north of Route 9 on the Long Trail, and the Goddard shelter 10.1 miles north of the highway.

Maps

For a map of hiking trails, refer to map 8 in the *Map and Guide to the Appalachian Trail in New Hampshire/Vermont,* an eight-map set and guidebook available for $19.95 ($14.95 for the maps alone) from the Appalachian Trail Conference. Or get the waterproof *End-to-End Map of the Long Trail,* available for $8.95 from the Green Mountain Club. For a topographic area map, request Woodford from USGS Map Sales, Federal Center, Box 25286, Denver, CO 80225, 888/ASK-USGS (888/275-8747), website: http://mapping.usgs.gov.

Directions

Drive to the large parking lot at the Long Trail/Appalachian Trail crossing of Route 9, 5.2 miles east of Bennington and 2.8 miles west of Woodford.

Contact

Green Mountain National Forest Supervisor, 231 North Main Street, Rutland, VT 05701, 802/747-6700, fax 802/747-6766, website: www.fs.fed.us/r9/gmfl. Green Mountain Club Inc., 4711 Waterbury-Stowe Road, Waterbury Center, VT 05677, 802/244-7037, website: www.greenmountainclub.org. Appalachian Trail Conference, 799 Washington Street, P.O. Box 807, Harpers Ferry, WV 25425-0807, 304/535-6331, website: www.appalachiantrail.org.

39 THE LONG TRAIL: MASSACHUSETTS LINE TO ROUTE 9

in the Green Mountain National Forest between Clarksburg, Massachusetts, and Woodford

Total distance: 14.2 miles one-way

Hiking time: 2 days

Difficulty: 6

Rating: 7

This southernmost stretch of the Long Trail—here coinciding with the Appalachian Trail—is for the most part an easy hike along a mostly flat, wooded ridge. The cumulative elevation gain is well under 1,000 feet per day. The southern Green Mountains are not known for spectacular views, although there are few on this hike. But this would be a good overnight backpacking trip for hikers who prefer a woods walk or for a beginner backpacker. Because the Long Trail's southern terminus lies in the forest on the Vermont-Massachusetts border, you have to access this hike via one of two trails, adding either 3.6 miles or 4 miles to this hike's distance.

The Pine Cobble Trail, the more interesting and slightly shorter of the two access trails, reaches the Long Trail in 3.6 miles; from the parking area, walk east on Brooks Road for 0.2 mile and turn left on Pine Cobble Road. The trail begins 0.1 mile up the road on the right and is marked by a sign.

The white-blazed Appalachian Trail takes four miles to reach the border of the two states, passing a view south to Mount Greylock from an old rock slide 2.4 miles from Route 2. From the state border, the Long Trail follows level, wooded terrain, crossing some old logging roads, for 2.6 miles to a junction with the Broad Brook Trail, which branches left (west) and leads four miles to a road outside Williamstown. At 2.8 miles, the Seth Warner Trail leads left (west) 0.2 mile to the Seth Warner shelter. Continuing north, the Long Trail crosses the dirt County Road at 3.1 miles, which connects Pownal and Stamford and may be passable by motor vehicle as far as the Long Trail. The Long Trail ascends several hundred feet over a 3,000-foot hill, drops down the other side, and then makes an easier climb over Consultation Peak (2,810 feet) before reaching Congdon Camp at 10 miles. At 10.5 miles, the Long Trail crosses the Dunville Hollow

Trail, which leads left (west) 0.7 mile to a rough woods road (turning right onto that road leads 1.8 miles to houses on Burgess Road and four miles to Route 9, a mile east of Bennington). The Long Trail follows more easy terrain before climbing slightly to the top of Harmon Hill (2,325 feet) at 12.5 miles, from which there are some views west toward Bennington and north toward Glastenbury Mountain. Continuing north, the trail descends at an easy grade for a mile, then drops steeply over the final half mile to Route 9.

User Groups

Hikers, snowshoers, and dogs. Dogs must be leashed. No wheelchair facilities. This trail is not suitable for skis. Bikes, horses, and hunting are prohibited.

Access and Fees

Parking and access are free. No-trace camping is permitted within the Green Mountain National Forest. The Seth Warner shelter is 300 yards west of the Long Trail, reached via a side path off the Long Trail, 2.8 miles north of the Massachusetts border. The Congdon Camp shelter is on the Long Trail, 10 miles north of the Massachusetts border and 4.3 miles south of Route 9.

Maps

For a map of hiking trails, refer to map 8 in the *Map and Guide to the Appalachian Trail in New Hampshire/Vermont,* an eight-map set and guidebook available for $19.95 ($14.95 for the maps alone) from the Appalachian Trail Conference. Or get the waterproof *End-to-End Map of the Long Trail,* available for $8.95 from the Green Mountain Club. For topographic area maps, request Pownal, Stamford, Bennington, and Woodford from USGS Map Sales, Federal Center, Box 25286, Denver, CO 80225, 888/ASK-USGS (888/275-8747), website: http://mapping.usgs.gov.

Directions

You need to shuttle two vehicles for this one-way traverse. To hike south to north, as described here, leave one vehicle in the large parking lot at the Long Trail/Appalachian Trail crossing of Route 9, 5.2 miles east of Bennington and 2.8 miles west of Woodford.

Then drive to one of two possible starts for this hike, both in Massachusetts. For the Pine Cobble start, from U.S. 7 in Williamstown, a mile south of the Vermont line and 0.3 mile north of the Hoosic River bridge, turn east on North Housac Road. Drive 0.5 mile and turn right on Brooks Road. Drive 0.7 mile and park in a dirt lot on the left marked by a sign reading, "Parking for Pine Cobble Trail." For the Appalachian Trail start, drive to the Appalachian Trail footbridge over the Hoosic River (where there is no convenient parking) on Route 2, 2.9 miles east of Williamstown center and 2.5 miles west of North Adams center.

Contact

Green Mountain National Forest Supervisor, 231 North Main Street, Rutland, VT 05701, 802/747-6700, fax 802/747-6766, website: www.fs.fed.us/r9/gmfl. Green Mountain Club Inc., 4711 Waterbury-Stowe Road, Waterbury Center, VT 05677, 802/244-7037, website: www.greenmountainclub.org. Appalachian Trail Conference, 799 Washington Street, P.O. Box 807, Harpers Ferry, WV 25425-0807, 304/535-6331, website: www.appalachiantrail.org.

Resources

COURTESY VERMONT DEPARTMENT OF TOURISM & MARKETING/DENNIS CURRAN

Resources

Public Lands Agencies

Green Mountain National Forest Supervisor
231 North Main Street
Rutland, VT 05701
802/747-6700, fax 802/747-6766
website: www.fs.fed.us/r9/gmfl

Vermont Department of Forests
Parks & Recreation
Commissioner's Office
103 South Main Street
Waterbury, VT 05671-0601
802/241-3655, fax 802/244-1481
website: www.state.vt.us/anr/fpr

Map Sources

DeLorme Publishing Company
800/253-5081
website: www.DeLorme.com

Trails Illustrated
800/962-1643
website: http://maps.national
geographic.com/trails

United States Geological Survey
Information Services
Box 25286
Denver, CO 80225
888/ASK-USGS (888/275-8747),
fax 303/202-4693
website: http://mapping
.usgs.gov

Trail Clubs and Organizations

Appalachian Trail Conference
799 Washington Street
P.O. Box 807
Harpers Ferry, WV 25425-0807
304/535-6331
website: www.appalachian
trail.org

Ascutney Trails Association
George Smith, Jr.
P.O. Box 119
Hartland, VT 05048

Green Mountain Club Inc.
4711 Waterbury-Stowe Road
Waterbury Center, VT 05677
802/244-7037, fax 802/244-5867
website: www.greenmountain
club.org

Acknowledgments

I want to thank the many people who accompanied me on these trails, in particular my wife and hiking partner, Penny Beach. My parents, Henry and Joanne Lanza, deserve recognition—both for putting up with a son who has shown up at their door a few times since they first got rid of him, and for being good hiking partners. I also want to thank my editors and the rest of the very talented staff at Avalon Travel Publishing.

While I have personally walked every hike described in this book—some of them many times—updating a volume as comprehensive as this one cannot possibly be accomplished without the assistance of many people. To that end, I relied on friends, acquaintances, people active with hiking and conservation groups, and managers of public lands and private reserves to do some on-the-ground "scouting" of trails and send me current reports on the hikes in this book. Much deep appreciation goes out to: Joe Albee, Mike and Rick Baron, Denise Buck, Steve Buck, Judy Glinder, Kellen Glinder, Carol Lavoie, Denis Lavoie, Peter Mahr, Bill Mistretta, Michele Morris, Gerry Prutsman, Christine Raymond, Lance Riek, Topher Sharp, and Doug Thompson.

There were also many helpful people at various organizations and public agencies, including: Appalachian Trail Conference; Ascutney Trails Association; Green Mountain Club; Green Mountain National Forest; Vermont Department of Forests, Parks, and Recreation.

Index

Notes